25
stupid
mistakes
parents
make

25 stupid mistakes parents make

Peter Jaksa, Ph.D.

ROXBURY PARK

LOWELL HOUSE
LOS ANGELES
NTC/Contemporary Publishing Group

Published by Lowell House
A division of NTC/Contemporary Publishing Group, Inc.
4255 West Touhy Avenue, Lincolnwood (Chicago), Illinois 60646-1975 U.S.A.
© 1998 by Lowell House

Lowell House books can be purchased at special discounts when ordered in
bulk for premiums and special sales. Contact Department CS at the following address:

NTC/Contemporary Publishing Group
4255 West Touhy Avenue
Lincolnwood, IL 60646-1975
1-800-323-4900

Library of Congress Cataloging-in-Publication Data

Jaksa, Peter.
    25 Stupid mistakes parents make / Peter Jaksa.
      p. cm.
    Includes bibliographical references and index.
    ISBN 0-7373-0121-X
      1. Child rearing. 2. Parent and child. 3. Parenting. I. Title.
    II. Title: Twenty five stupid mistakes parents make.
    HQ769.J294   1999
    649'.1—dc21   99-13523
                                          CIP

Roxbury Park is a division of NTC/Contemporary Publishing Group, Inc.

Managing Director and Publisher: Jack Artenstein
Editor in Chief, Roxbury Park Books: Michael Artenstein
Director of Publishing Services: Rena Copperman
Editorial Assistant: Nicole Monastirsky
Interior Designer: Andrea Reider

Printed and bound in the United States of America
99 00 01 02 03 04 DHD 10 9 8 7 6 5 4 3 2 1

This book is dedicated to:

My daughter Jennifer,
who has taught me as much as I have taught her.

My wife Susan,
who has managed parenthood and career artfully.

Matei Jaksa, Anuica Jaksa, Jacqueline Roberti, and
Dominick Roberti, our parents, who have shown the way
with love, guidance, humor, and affection. May their influence
be passed along to countless others who read this book.

Contents

Introduction

"I'm a parent—now what?"

There are no perfect parents.

Good, we got that out of the way. Trying to be a perfect parent makes as much sense as trying to have perfect children. It creates unreasonable pressures and a sense of failure and inadequacy. It is an expectation doomed to failure, and before it fails it will make your life miserable.

Let's be realistic from the outset: being a good parent does not require perfection, but it does require doing the right things as a parent most of the time. The "right" things involve a combination of love, discipline, teaching, and guidance, a process that goes on from birth to adulthood—and in some ways even in adulthood. Being a parent is a job that we never outgrow. This book is about learning, and doing, those fundamental "right" things that make good parents and help raise healthy children. Good parenting requires strong helpings of love, patience, common sense, the ability to learn and adapt, and the willingness to provide guidance and discipline even through the toughest times while your children are growing up. Do that consistently enough and you will earn your parent wings. This book can help lay the groundwork for being a very good parent.

The bad news is, it is also very possible to be a *bad* parent. Bad parenting comes in part from neglecting to do what responsible parents need to do. Bad parenting also comes from doing some truly horrendous, destructive things that damage children, marriages, and families. This book is also about avoiding the serious mistakes that can cause real and lasting harm. Sometimes the mistakes parents make are not intentional at all, and may even be the result of very good intentions. Few if any parents say to themselves, "well, we're about to get divorced, why don't we tear the kids to pieces emotionally in the process?" The intent to hurt the children may not be there, but it is sad and disturbing how often hurting children is the result. If you're a parent with young children and contemplating divorce, please read chapter 19: The Perils of Divorce. Don't do the things I ask divorced parents not to do, and you (and your children) will come out far ahead. Some parenting "mistakes" are too serious to ignore or tiptoe around. If this book can prevent even one or two of these mistakes in the lives of your children, then it will serve its purpose.

This book is not about gimmicks. Communication or relationship gimmicks are not required for good parenting, and in fact may be a detriment to honesty, respect, and trust. The search for gimmicks is usually related to the desire for a quick fix or a magical solution. Good parents know instinctively that there are no quick fixes or hocus pocus for the challenges of parenting and the many problems children may encounter in growing up. Good parenting takes dedication, enormous amounts of caring, and perseverance in doing what you know is right even when you want to give up or believe that things are hopeless. Good parenting takes knowledge and lots of work. This book can provide some of the knowledge. You have to provide the work.

Good parenting does not happen in isolation. The best parenting happens within a family where affection, trust, and respect flourish. This is a recurrent theme that I found myself coming back to while writing many of the chapters in this book. It does not matter if a family consists of two people or ten, the quality of relationships within that family is crucial to the well-being of every person. A healthy family makes for fewer serious parent-child problems, and often makes parenting a joyous occasion. An unhealthy family can make the parent's job much, much more difficult. The importance of the family, and things that parents can do to strengthen their families, is something that is touched on often in this book and for very good reason. Being part of a close family involves giving, sharing, being honest about good and bad things, sacrificing, nurturing, and supporting each other. Every relationship is enriched under those conditions, not the least the parent-child relationship.

In closing I must offer thanks to my own parents, who struggled under tremendously difficult conditions at times to raise seven children into responsible and caring adults. Their ability to overcome challenges and adversity, and keep the family together and strong through it all, has earned my respect and admiration for them as individuals and for the importance of good parenting in general. I would also like to thank the several hundred families and parents with whom I have worked over the past twenty years. Each family is unique in its own way, yet all share the same common needs for cooperation, security, belonging and closeness. I have learned something from each of them. I hope that some of the collective wisdom is returned and communicated to others who read this book.

PETER JAKSA, PH.D.
Northbrook, Illinois

Chapter **1**

Who's in Charge Here Anyway?

Adults marry so they can love and be loved, share their resources, and often to raise a family. A "good" marriage involves spouses who support and respect each other, and try to work cooperatively as equals. The partners complement each other rather than competing or working on conflicting agendas. Feelings of intimacy and trust within a marriage are highly correlated with shared power, and it's usually a bad idea to have one partner try to dominate the other. A good marriage, in other words, is very much a democratic process. When children are added to the mix, however, the situation stops being as clear or straightforward.

DON'T GIVE UP YOUR PARENTAL AUTHORITY

Should the kids become part of the democratic process? To what degree can they be treated as "equals" within the family equation? These are questions many parents struggle with as they figure out what it means to be a parent, and what kind of parent one wants to be. The issue becomes more complicated when some prominent child-rearing experts recommend that, why of course, children *should* be treated as equals. Aren't their needs just as important as the parents' needs? Furthermore, the argument goes, if children are treated as inferiors, their self-esteem will suffer and they will resent the parents for being controlling. Disagreements between parent and child should be dealt with via communication and negotiation whenever possible. Children should be given choices, not told what to do. How else will they learn to make decisions on their own and grow up to be responsible adults?

The Limits of Family Democracy

As appealing as this "democratic" view of parenthood may be for many parents, it has practical as well as theoretical limitations. If carried too far, the end result will likely be a guilt-ridden parent who is repeatedly jumping through hoops in an effort to be fair. The child, on their end, may lack a strong sense of security and end up feeling confused and overwhelmed rather than empowered.

I have worked with hundreds of parents and children, and most of them intuitively recognize the universal truth that the parent-child relationship is not one between equals, unlike the ideal marital relationship discussed above. Psychologists Melvin Silberman and Susan Wheelan also make this point in their book *How to Discipline Without Feeling Guilty* when they note: "As much as we like to think that a family or classroom functions as a democracy, children correctly perceive that there is a power hierarchy to which they must ultimately accommodate themselves." This is a reasonable and realistic statement about the role of authority in the parent-child relationship. Most kids will challenge the parents' authority at some point, but if the parents hold firm, their authority will be respected. This tends to work out best for both parent and child.

Parents and kids don't occupy the same level in the family's authority structure, nor should they. Children within a family have equal rights to be loved, respected, and have their needs provided for. This does *not* imply equal rights in making decisions, determining goals, or resolving conflicts. Not everything in life can be a choice, and not every problem can be mediated.

Why Parents Need to Be in Charge

Children play an equal role in the love and caring that goes on within a family, but they also need protection, teaching, guidance, and discipline. To use an old-fashioned word, they need to be raised. Children need to know that their parents are in charge. This does not imply acting in a domineering and controlling manner, but as strong adults who can deal with dangers and difficulties, provide for the family's needs, and make the right decisions on important matters. This is what promotes a sense of emotional security and safety for the child, not the opportunity to negotiate with the parents or treating their parents as equals. For practical, safety, and health reasons, parents have to be in charge. When this is understood and accepted by both parents and children, trust and cooperation rise rather than diminish. Parents who abdicate their authority as parents, no matter how good their intentions might be, invite more conflicts, insecurity, and problems for themselves and their children.

Children Are Children   By the very nature of childhood, children are emotionally immature, self-centered, impulsive, and demanding. This does not in any way mean that children are "bad," but simply that they are indeed children. If an adult acts selfishly, demandingly, and causes a scene by overreacting emotionally, we might say that she is "acting like a child" and mean that as a criticism. If the person *is* a child, that behavior is normal for a certain age level and should be expected at times. Children need to be taught responsible, healthy, appropriate behaviors, because, as every parent knows, they are certainly not born with good judgment or all the social graces.

Raising our children, or, in more formal terms, socializing them, involves teaching them a wide variety of knowledge and skills. These include responsibility, respect for rules and authority, the art of planning and thinking things through, delaying gratification and working for larger goals, and respect and consideration for others. Learning mature behaviors involves a long series of lessons over many years, taught in large part by caring and attentive parents who can set rules, enforce limits, and provide both love and discipline. The parents are clearly in the position of teachers, guides, and, yes, even bosses when necessary, and not in a position of equality that characterizes a friendship. A true friendship between parent and child is likely not possible until the child becomes an adult. Before that the child needs something much more important—a parent!

The Lessons of Rules, Limits, and Protection

Children need rules and limits, and indeed thrive on them. That does not mean the child will *like* your rules or readily accept the limits you set, so be prepared to be challenged. You as the parent are guaranteed to hear many times how unfair your rules are, and how none of your child's friends have parents who are so mean! Nevertheless, the rules and limits, fairly enforced, are crucial to your child's well-being and your peace of mind. If you allow a child a great deal of "choice" in the matters of food, curfew, chores, and homework, for example, you may well end up with a child who lives on junk food, stays up late, and gets around to doing her homework when she gets tired of playing video games or watching TV. Chores? You have got to be kidding. Who has time for chores these days? The role of the parent is to provide guidance, supervision, and, when necessary, discipline to ensure that these fundamental things get done.

Our responsibilities as parents are to provide for, protect, and teach our children. These are best carried out with love and understanding, but they do not have to be an exercise in guilt and should never be underestimated in importance. All children are dependent on their parents, particularly when young. This dependency is sensed on an emotional level by the child even though it may not be verbalized. At a basic survival level, children depend on their adult caretakers for food, shelter, clothing, and the simple necessities of life including a place within the family. When that basic support is missing, sadly and often tragically, children turn to gangs, cults, or street life, which involve drug and crime subcultures.

The role of protecting children still falls primarily to parents and adult caretakers. Although many social agencies serve a protective function in our society, they cannot be a substitute for caring parents. The job of educating children and teaching them life skills is ours as parents. Schools play an important role of course, but schools cannot duplicate the personal and emotional impact parents have on their children's emotional and moral development. Parents still make the most influential teachers for their children, and always will.

An Assertive Parent Is Not a Dictator, Marshmallow, or Guilt Monger

Now that we have praised the values of parents asserting their authority, what *about* the needs of children to make choices and exercise freedoms in their lives? Certainly this is an important part of growing up and getting along with each other as family members. The short answer is that children should be expected to be responsible for, and make choices in, the things in life they can handle. What those things are will depend partly on the child's age and maturity level. The long answer is that parents play a crucial part in determining just which freedoms and choices the child is capable of making at that point in his life. What are appropriate, realistic, healthy expectations and choices for a particular child can be discussed and negotiated to some degree, but bottom line, the parents have to act in the child's best interests. This is not a matter of control, but of responsibility.

Affective Parenting Is Not About Control Nor is it about abdicating authority. The fear of being too controlling and thus stifling their children's growth has caused untold numbers of parents to become passive, self-doubting, and permissive in their relationships with their children. As noted above, this is not a good situation for either the parent or child. Permissive and passive parents become figurative "marshmallows" who cave in to guilt and pressure in order to avoid conflicts. What the child is likely to learn from that type of interaction is that guilt trips pay off, and putting up a fight gets results. The well-intentioned parents bending over backward in an effort to be "fair" and "supporting" ends up in an ongoing struggle with a child who regards them as more of a sibling to be competed with rather than a parent to be respected and obeyed. The outcome will be more guilt trips, more pressure, and more manipulation.

The Intimidating Parent

There are parents who are too controlling of course, but this falls in the category of being intimidating and dictatorial, not assertive. As Drs. Silberman and Wheelan note in *How to Discipline Without Feeling Guilty*, some parents use intimidation or guilt to frighten or bully children into doing their will. These methods are always destructive and should not be used. Intimidation threatens the child's safety and self-esteem, and may produce meek compliance or passive-aggressive rebellion.

The dictatorial parent who expects the child to follow their every wish is certainly not acting in the child's best interests, and consequently not acting responsibly as a parent. An aggressive, intimidating parent is often a person with a need to overcome their own sense of weakness and inferiority by coercing or intimidating a child. An assertive parent always keeps the child's needs and welfare in mind, and bases his or her behavior toward the child on what will benefit the child.

Guilt Tactics

The parent who uses guilt tactics to get the child to comply is avoiding conflict and responsibility in a different manner. Telling the child how much their behavior hurts the parent, for example, may produce some changes in the child's behavior but also leaves the child feeling shamed, even questioning their self-worth. If a child is made to feel like a "bad" child because of conflicts with the parents, or because some task such as cleaning her room did not get carried out, the emotional damage caused can be far worse than the actual problem behaviors.

Parents using guilt tactics may be unaware that they are doing so. Perhaps the parents were also subjected to such behaviors when they were growing up, and the guilt-inducing tactics may seem "natural" to them. It should always be kept in mind, however, that statements and behaviors directed at children which criticize, belittle, and shame are harmful to self-esteem and damage the emotional bond between the parent and child. It is much healthier for the parents to express their needs and wishes to the child directly, and impose rewards and punishments in responding to the child's behavior without resorting to criticism, blame, or guilt.

Using Parental Authority Responsibly

Parental authority needs to be respected by children of course, but also needs to be acknowledged and respected by the parents as well. The problems that I sometimes see in working with families is not always that children refuse to respect their parents, but that oftentimes parents feel guilty, embarrassed, or confused about asserting their parental authority in positive ways. Indeed it takes some persuading before they can accept that an assertive parent is not a dictator, controlling, or some kind of abusive ogre. Assertive parenting loves, teaches, and guides. Passive, guilt-driven parenting provides a lax atmosphere and leaves children to drift to places that don't provide for emotional security and may even be dangerous.

Set Limits, But Choose Your Battles   There are limits to parental authority of course, and to what it can accomplish. It's important to recognize when asserting authority may be counterproductive, or simply not enough for what the child needs. Parents should not try to have everything their way, particularly as children grow older and reach adolescence. Woe to the parent who tries to be controlling with a teenager striving to establish her sense of independence, because that will quickly become an eternal battle and power struggle. Parental authority needs to be applied most when important matters are at stake, with greater freedom allowed for the child to make decisions as maturity increases. If violent or abusive behavior develops, it's time for professional help and intervention. Some problems that children develop, such as emotional problems, or problems with alcohol and other drug abuse, also require professional intervention and cannot be handled by good parenting alone. The wise parent knows when to call in the troops.

Where does good parenting start? It actually begins with a strong, loving relationship between the parents themselves. This promotes feelings of security and stability. The strength of this security need for the children is sometimes made painfully clear in their opposition to any plans their parents might have about splitting up or divorcing. Beyond providing security, the parents need to provide guidance and structure. This may involve some thinking and planning about exactly what kind of parent you want to be. You the parent must set the rules, goals, and expectations about how things are done in your family. Make those rules and expectations realistic and clear, enforce them fairly, and your children will respect them, you, and themselves.

Chapter **2**

Be Available to Your Children

A s every new parent soon learns, most children have a constant need for attention, reassurance, and love. Their sense of emotional security and their sense of worth is tied in important and intimate ways to the time and attention given to them by their parents or other primary caregivers. Children also have a universal fear of abandonment. This fear can be particularly intense when children are young, but also lasts well into the teenage years.

DON'T BE THE "ABSENT PARENT"

Children learn that parents are not always around, and that life involves painful and sometimes unexpected loss. They see friends losing parents through death, caused by illness or accidents. Even more frequently, they see other children losing their parents through divorce. Some children develop separation anxiety, a persistent and unrealistic fear that something bad will happen to the parents. The fear of losing a parent, in itself, may cause increased stress for the child on top of life's usual stressors. When loss of a parent occurs, children react with depression and anxiety.

Who Is the Absent Parent?

The loss of a parent, which many children experience, may not necessarily involve physical loss, such as that caused by death or divorce.

Often the loss involves an emotional loss caused by a parent who is not available to that child. This is the "absent parent." Many parents remain part of the child's family, but are physically absent due to being involved too much in their work or other activities, or are simply emotionally unavailable. For the child the results are the same: a sense of abandonment, emotional deprivation, a decreased sense of importance and worth. If the abandonment continues, it is common to see children react with anger, acting out behaviors, and physical and emotional withdrawal on their end. At that point, the parent has lost one of the most intimate and precious things he can ever hope to have, namely the love and respect of his child.

Denial of the Absent Parent   The tragedy of the "absent parent" is as sad as it is preventable. Most parents would shake their heads in disbelief at the possibility that they would become unavailable to the children they love. Not I, they decry! Even if their own parent was too busy with work, or escaping through alcohol and other drugs, or lost in untreated and poorly managed emotional illness, few parents would allow that they will treat their own children in that manner. One problem of course is that emotional abandonment of a child is not always intentional, and may not even be recognized by the parent. At other times, a parent may be so self-absorbed in their own interests that the child's needs go unrecognized and unheeded. The story of Lewis provides an example of what can happen when a parent loses touch with the meaning and responsibilities of parenthood.

Lewis's Story

Lewis was nine years old when his parents divorced. He loved them both and wished desperately that they could get along, but that was never to be. After too many arguments, several broken dishes which his mother threw against the kitchen wall, and fearful evenings of hiding in the den with his little brother while the battle raged between the adults, their father, Mike, moved out of the house. The relief over having an end to their parents' arguments was tempered by the fact that their father, who had been spending too much time at the office anyway, was now even less available to them.

Lewis never felt very close to his father but craved desperately his father's approval. Mike had been a college football player and was a successful executive at his company. He played golf regularly and had a busy social life. Lewis was bored to death by golf but took lessons anyway and played once a month in order to spend time with his father. They had a buddy-buddy relationship on the golf course. At least Lewis had this time with his father, which was more than his brother Darren had who was only five at the time. The boys enjoyed being with their mother, who was a loving and attentive parent, but always looked forward to visiting their dad on weekends. They would go see a ball game or movie, or golf.

Remarriage Blues   Four months after their parents' separation, Lewis was shocked to learn that his father was getting remarried shortly. His father's fiancée moved into his apartment and quickly made it clear that this was now her home. When the boys visited on weekends she restricted TV times, and sent them to bed early if they misbehaved. The adults started going out regularly on weekend nights, leaving the boys with a babysitter. When Lewis complained about this to his father, he was told not to be selfish and to think about the needs of his soon-to-be stepmom who got bored with staying home. Lewis became increasingly more angry and resentful with Lisa, the fiancée, who was apparently stealing his father away. It did not help matters when his mother indicated, indirectly but unmistakably, that Lisa was to blame for the parents' divorce. At that point Lewis declared behavioral war.

Misreading the Child's Needs

Mike's reaction to his son's rebellious behavior toward Lisa was to clamp down harder on Lewis. He chastised the boy for his lack of respect, and cut back on their golfing trips. When both boys complained that it was no longer fun to visit their father, their visits were cut back to every other weekend. Mike was busier at work now due to a promotion and also preoccupied with his fiancée and the marriage plans. Lewis's anger turned to sadness as he realized that he lost the battle for his father's affection. He moped around the house more and spent his time watching TV. He spent less time with his friends, and eventually they stopped calling as much.

Lewis's grades dropped in school because he was not trying as hard. The school problems caught the attention of both his parents and teachers. His mother pleaded with Lewis to apply himself more, and promised him a new video game set. His father gave him a lecture about being a winner or a loser and what it took to be a winner in life. When Lewis came home after that particular visit, his mother could see the dejection written all over his face. "I love dad but he can be such a jerk," Lewis said dejectedly. She found it difficult to disagree.

Partial Solutions

Lewis was taken to see a therapist due to his depression and falling academic performance. Mike declined to attend, citing his work demands and the mother's putting the blame on him for their son's problems. He indicated however that he would do his share by paying for the sessions. The therapy gave Lewis a safe and creative outlet for his feelings of anger and resentment toward his father. He still had a desperate want for his father's affection and acceptance but was rapidly losing hope that he could obtain it. Although he still loved his father, Lewis became increasingly distanced from him as a way of protecting himself emotionally from the pain of his father's self-absorption.

Following his father's marriage to Lisa, and the birth of their own daughter, Lewis became more reluctant to visit with them and often found excuses to cancel the visits. Sadly, there was not to be a happy ending to this story. When two years later Mike got transferred by his company to a different state, it made things easier to bear for the son. At least Lewis now had a legitimate excuse for why his father was not a part of his life. For his part, Mike had lost his oldest son.

The Children's Divorce   When Lewis's parents became divorced, they divorced each other of course and not the children. Both had continuing obligations in their roles as parents, and were very much needed by their young children. Mike the father abdicated his responsibilities as a parent by involving himself in a narcissistic manner in his work, his interests, and his fiancée who eventually became his new wife. The loss for Lewis was not limited to losing the security of their family, brought on by the divorce, but also compounded by being further abandoned emotionally by his father. After a period of anger and rebelliousness, followed by helplessness and depression, the boy in turn detached emotionally from the father. Some of the anger and sadness stayed with him, buried deep where it might do the least amount of damage, and therefore most likely to stay with the boy for a very long time.

The Overworked Parent

Why would parents abandon their children? In her book *Fast Forwarding Through Childhood*, Mary Zesiewic, M.D., cites four common ways that this could happen. First, some parents simply work too hard and too long and are not physically available. When they are physically present, they often are exhausted and don't have much energy or patience for their children. These parents often love their children and have the best intentions, but get preoccupied with their work responsibilities. People who work at professional or executive jobs, those who are self-employed, and single mothers who have to balance work and family responsibilities are particularly vulnerable to become overwhelmed by or overinvolved with their work. The solution of course is to carve out time for the family and stick to those "family times." Often what the children need most is simply for the parent to be around more. The relationship will take care of itself.

The Sick Parent

A second reason for absentee parenthood is sickness or disability. This may involve an extended physical illness, a chronic emotional illness such as severe depression or schizophrenia, or a problem with alcohol and drug abuse. In these circumstances, the parent may be willing to be more involved with the children's lives but simply incapable of doing so. The sense of loss on the children's part can be great, regardless of the reason for the problem.

When psychological or emotional problems are present, it is the parent's responsibility to seek appropriate and effective treatment and thus manage the problem as well as possible. Having a history of depression, schizophrenia, bipolar disorder, or other types of emotional disability does not preclude anyone from being a responsible, loving parent. The emotional problem may make parenting more difficult, but certainly not impossible. If substance abuse is a problem for the parent, that parent has an urgent responsibility to seek appropriate treatment for herself and manage the problem. A parent who is abusing alcohol or other drugs will not only be emotionally unavailable to the child, but may also pose a serious health risk to his children due to substandard childcare and the increased risk of having car accidents and other misfortunes.

The Self-Absorbed Parent

A third cause of parents emotionally abandoning their children is when the parents are too absorbed in their own goals and interests and neglect the child's needs. These tend to be the narcissistic parents, such as Mike, the father in the previous story. Unfortunately, some aspects of our culture encourage people to pursue their own needs first, regardless of the cost to others. This "looking out for No. 1" philosophy is taken literally to mean that selfishness and self-absorption are acceptable or even desirable.

Some people have what is called narcissistic personality disorder, which truly involves an inability to empathize with other people, to be aware of their needs, or care about their needs. As disturbing as it may sound, this personality defect can even apply to parents and their children. The opposite extreme to the narcissistic parent is the parent who devotes her life to the children, at the expense of considering her own needs or interests. This is not a healthy situation for the parents or children either of course. The solution is to find a balance between the parent's needs and the children's needs, where the parent does not assume the role of either the narcissist or the martyr.

The Overwhelmed Parent

A fourth condition where parents abandon their children emotionally is when one or both parents are too overwhelmed by marital problems and strife to be able to attend to their children's needs. If the marital problems become long-term, the marriage takes on a toxic quality which is emotionally destructive for everyone. These parents are simply too chronically angry and upset to be sensitive or attentive to their children, and too stressed emotionally to provide much nurturance. If alcohol abuse or other drug abuse is involved, the problem is compounded and made much worse. This situation simply begs for marital therapy or family therapy. If the problems are not resolved, the solution may well be a divorce. It is not true, as had been commonly believed even twenty years ago, that it's best to keep a marriage together "for the sake of the children." Children can be harmed more by being a part of a conflictual, toxic marriage than by divorce.

What Parents Can Do

The keys to maintaining close, nurturing relationships with your children are within the reach of every parent, but they must be put into practice. To start with, make yourself available to your children! That means spending time with them, showing interest in their activities, and doing recreational or fun things on a regular basis. This is particularly true when the children are young, but even applies during the teen years. The interest must be genuine, not faked. Children are very sensitive to parents' reasons for doing things with them, and will resent the parent who does things out of a sense of obligation or guilt.

When it comes down to it, it really does not matter whether you are busy at work or trying to improve your golf game. If you don't have time for your children, and have a genuine interest and affection for them, you must ask why in heaven did you bother having children in the first place? And the answer: what is your intention now? Every parent, upon becoming a parent, assumes the responsibility of finding the time and interest to be involved in her children's lives. There are no exceptions, and no good excuses.

Ties That Bind and Nurture

Families require cohesion to ensure the well-being and emotional security of its members, and particularly that of the children. When a parent becomes too busy, preoccupied, overwhelmed, or self-absorbed to attend to a child's needs, the cohesion breaks down. Intimacy is lost, trust is broken, and the loss of emotional security can be devastating. It is tremendously important in these hectic times to make room for family time, and keep it holy. Establishing routines and traditions helps build stability and security. Eating meals together establishes family bonds that last a lifetime. Celebrating certain holidays and anniversaries builds traditions and a sense of family identity.

Most important, taking some time day in and day out to talk, show interest, ask questions, and show affection, builds emotional bonds that last and can withstand the problems and pressures that life often places on families and individuals. Attention and love that are faxed in, phoned in, E-mailed, or expressed through a toy or a check are not enough. These are nice gestures when done occasionally, but not a substitute for spending time together. Children require your presence. The lucky parent who makes time for this benefits as much as does the lucky child.

Chapter **3**

Violence, Danger, and Disasters, Oh My

Without a doubt, the world can be a scary place for both children and adults. What can make things worse is if we overemphasize the negative and scary things to such a degree that we make the world *appear* to be more scary and dangerous than it really is. The end result is that we scare ourselves to excess, beyond what is realistic or healthy. In particular, we can scare our children senseless.

DON'T MAKE THE WORLD A SCARY PLACE

An impressionable child who is subjected to thousands of images of violence, crime, and disasters, and cautioned hundreds of times by well-meaning parents, teachers, and other responsible adults, can easily form a perception of the world that it is unsafe and cannot be trusted. If we exaggerate and overemphasize the dangers, we risk creating a generation of emotionally stressed-out children who grow up afraid and insecure.

Dangers versus Phobias

Realistic dangers need to be dealt with in realistic ways without exaggeration. We want our children to be cautious of strangers who show undue interest in them, but do we want them to be fearful of every adult they meet? We want them to understand why doors should be locked when the family goes to sleep at night, but do we want them to lie in their beds being fearful of burglars breaking in? Children should be taught about the real dangers of tornadoes and lightning storms, for example, and the precautions they should take during bad weather. Does that mean that we want our children to be scared of every dark cloud that comes up in the sky? Of course not. The children would live in a perpetual state of fear of bad weather (as a matter of fact, I have met some children with precisely that fear). Not every cloud harbors a lightning bolt, and not every person is a likely kidnapper or abuser. Overblown fears result in the "Chicken Little" perception of the world seeming realistic, and "Stranger Danger" running amok. Children who perceive their environment as dangerous and threatening are more likely to develop stress-related disorders, anxiety, phobias, and somatic problems.

The Story of Angela: A Girl with Fears

Angela is seven years old. She has big brown eyes which look directly at you during a conversation. Angela has a number of fears which make it tough for her peace of mind, as well as her sense of security and safety. She's afraid of the dark, spiders, and dogs. She's afraid that other kids won't like her. She's afraid of something bad happening to her parents, which she worries about very much. She's afraid of someone breaking into the house at night, and worries about this constantly. She has nightmares about the house catching on fire. Because of her fears she often has to sleep with her parents. Angela is afraid to sleep over at a friend's house, and she turned down an opportunity to attend a church-sponsored summer camp. She gets stomachaches and headaches, more than most kids her age. She stays home from school more than most kids because she's not feeling well.

Today Angela is upset with her mother. "My mother deserted me," she says, and her eyes widen with disbelief. As Angela explains, she went with her mother to the grocery store, the same store they've been going to since Angela was an infant. It's a large, well-lit, chain grocery store in a peaceful suburban neighborhood. It's usually bustling with people and very busy. As Angela described it, she and her mother were going up and down the aisles. She was scanning items on the shelves and making suggestions to her mother. She has her favorite cereals, and always stops by the candy section. While Angela scans the shelves she also scans the people around her. She stays close to her mother, particularly when other people pass by.

While Angela was looking at rows of cracker and cookie boxes, her mother told her that she forgot to pick up mouthwash and went back to the last aisle. The girl was too preoccupied to hear her. Seconds later Angela looked up, and to her horror her mother was gone! Panic quickly set in. She yelled for her mother, her voice irritated and apprehensive, which attracted the attention of several people nearby. A store employee ran over to see what was wrong, but she refused to speak to him. Angela's mother quickly returned, carrying the bottle of mouthwash she had forgotten earlier. "What's wrong, sweetie?" the mother asked. Angela was relieved to see her, but also clearly angry. "How could you leave me all alone?" she asked her mother with hurt in her voice. Her underlying message to her mother was very clear: how could you place me in such danger?

Oversensitive Children Did Angela overreact? Her mother thought so, because Angela was in no danger while the mother walked over one aisle to get an item. Angela of course felt differently. Most important, she felt abandoned and *unsafe.* Her mother leaving her side was the last straw in her pile of anxiety, which was related to her perception of the store being unsafe and the people around her being scary and threatening. Later that day Angela's aunt scolded the mother for leaving the child unattended, even for a minute. Who knows what might happen in a minute? Disaster can strike at any time, and there are stories in the media of children being abducted in broad daylight from public places. Angela's father made a joke about having to sell her Barbie doll collection to pay her ransom if she was kidnapped. Angela didn't think that was very funny!

Who was right in that situation? Realistically, children should not be left unattended in public places. At the same time, it's difficult to argue that Angela was placed in danger by her mother's behavior. The chances of a stranger kidnapping her in a grocery store isle, with her mother close by, and walking out of the store with her without Angela screaming bloody murder and alerting other people, was very remote to say the least. Certainly it did not warrant being afraid of the grocery store, of the people shopping in the store, or of losing sight of her mother for a minute. It could be argued that the biggest problem in that situation was Angela's fear of being abandoned, her exaggerated sense of danger, and her panicked reaction when she lost sight of her mother.

Real Dangers, or Hype?

At this point I can almost hear some parents' protests. Children should not be left unwatched! There are fiends roaming amongst us! It is certainly true that there are some sick individuals in our society who prey on children, and will trick children into going with them, or even forcefully kidnap them. Children need to be made aware that such dangers exist, and they should be taught some ways in which to deal with the situation should it ever arise. Responsible parents have always taught their children that you don't go with a stranger, don't accept candy or toys from somebody trying to entice you, and don't get into somebody's car. If somebody tries to coerce you into going with them, you run, yell, make noise, go into a public place and ask for help, ring a neighbor's doorbell, and so on. These are realistic precautions which teach children how to recognize and deal with real dangers. They should be discussed with children in a calm and factual manner, not in an atmosphere of anxiety and dread. The vast majority of people "out there" are responsible and well-intentioned people.

More Danger or More Awareness? Are our communities really more dangerous than they were thirty, forty, or fifty years ago? Our perceptions of our communities *is* certainly more negative, due in no small part to repeated images of violence, dangers, and disasters which bombard us through the mass media on a daily basis. Dinnertime has become a time for the evening news and a fresh series of stories about murders, tornadoes, plane crashes, and so on. TV news shows, newspapers, and movies provide a relentless display of the problems and dangers in the world. Not coincidentally, repeated exposure to violent, dangerous, scary images goes hand in hand with our perceptions of the world as a scary and dangerous place.

In a Child's Eye

Young children are particularly impressionable since they don't have the intellectual maturity and sophistication to place events in a broader perspective. An earthquake in Los Angeles seems just as threatening to a child in Detroit when viewed repeatedly on the family's TV set. A shooting incident between neighbors miles away may cast doubt about the sanity and homicidal potential of Mr. and Mrs. Jones next door. Not only do bad things happen, but often these tragedies are widely publicized. People get shot, die in violent accidents, and burn up in houses that have caught fire. Pictures of the victims flash on the screen, usually taken from family photos or school graduation pictures. These unfortunate people are typically normal, average people who look just like you and me. The message gets absorbed in the child's mind: this could be you. You could be next. Maybe not today, or even tomorrow, but someday you could be shot, crash in an airplane or car, drown in a flood, have your house torn up by a tornado, or die of smoke inhalation when your house catches on fire. Or, you could be kidnapped. It happens every day, and they show it on the six o'clock news. No one is safe, and there is no place to run.

Exaggerated Fears A healthy solution to exaggerated fears is of course to provide a realistic view of the world we live in, and the people who inhabit that world. The TV news is part of the entertainment media, and not an accurate or typical reflection of the world. Freddie Kruger only exists in slasher movies. There are some very sick individuals who prey on children, but those are the exception and not the rule. Most people are your teachers, doctors, neighbors, and relatives. An adult who behaves inappropriately or in a threatening manner should be reported to a parent or other responsible adult. Although some children are kidnapped by total strangers, this is rare, and most incidents of child abduction involve a relative in a divorce situation where custody is disputed. A child is more likely to suffer abuse at the hands of a family member or someone else they know, and not from a stranger off the street.

Children need to be taught about behavior which can be inappropriate and harmful, whatever the source of that behavior is. Just as important, children need to be taught precautions and what to do when faced with realistic dangers. Don't tell someone who calls on the phone that you're home alone, for example. Children should be taught how to call 911 for emergencies, or to call a neighbor. A child should not answer the door when a parent is not home. Learn how to say "no" to an adult in an assertive manner, and seek help from other adults if necessary. What should the child do if she or he gets lost? Discuss the options the child can pursue. A family should practice fire escape routines, and agree on where to meet outside so that everyone is accounted for. Preparing for realistic dangers makes them less scary, and leaves the children feeling safer and the parents less worried. A child who is equipped with awareness of realistic dangers and the coping skills to handle potential problems need not be afraid of people, public places, or the world in general.

When Parents Should Worry

Parents should be concerned if their child shows symptoms of being excessively stressed, anxious, or afraid. These children may become more withdrawn and clingy, afraid to venture out from their parents' company. While this separation anxiety is common and considered normal in very young children, it can be quite a problem in older children and affect their emotional and social development. Overstressed children may cry more, refuse to cooperate, or become moody, angry, and destructive. An increase in somatic symptoms such as headaches, stomachaches, and difficulty sleeping may be evident. Chronic stress can result in long-term problems such as depression, juvenile onset diabetes, hypertension, a lower functioning immune system, and many other physical problems. High levels of anxiety often impair social relationships, the ability to trust and establish intimacy, and school and job performance. When anxiety, fears, and stress get out of hand, it's a good idea to consult a therapist who works with children and families. Therapy can benefit not only the child, but also the parents and the entire family.

Chapter **4**

Communicate with Children on Their Level

From the moment they're born, all children communicate with the world around them. They respond to people and events around them in somewhat different ways as they get older and more mature. The familiar parental lament of "they grow up so fast!" also reflects the reality that "they change so quickly!" As our children mature in their thinking, feelings, interests, and independence, it is the parents' job to keep up with them and adapt to their level of maturity. What worked for a parent when the child was five won't work at age ten, and what worked at ten won't work at age fifteen.

DON'T EXPECT THE SAME THINGS AT DIFFERENT AGES

As new parents soon discover, young children communicate to us via their emotional states. Their first expressions may be angry cries because they are hungry, wet, too hot, or too cold. The baby's cries send a clear message even though no words are exchanged. Expressions of discomfort and anger are universally understood by children and parents. Even children a few weeks old are capable of producing a smile and showing pleasure. What the infant communicates are feeling states, and most parents quickly become tuned in to them and try to respond appropriately. It is important for the parents to respond with words and feelings as well, not just behavior. The parents' expression of feelings provide reassurance and emotional comfort for even the youngest baby.

Recognize the Feeling State

What is true for infants is also true for toddlers and older children as well. Because their verbal abilities are underdeveloped, they communicate things to us through feelings and behaviors. As obvious as this seems for the six-month-old or twelve-month-old child, it also holds true for the six-year-old and even the twelve-year-old. Even when verbal skills are more developed and the child can put thoughts and feelings into words, it still remains important to pay attention to the underlying feeling state and respond to that. Often the words spoken by the child are not the real message, and don't reflect the real issue or the child's true feelings. Many times what is necessary is to acknowledge the child's feelings and respond to them before the real story can come out.

It is important for young children to simply be able to identify their feelings. A child may feel "all mixed up inside" but not really understand what the feelings are. This is particularly true when they have ambivalent or mixed feelings about something. At that point it can be very useful for a parent to reflect feelings back to the child, thus giving the feeling a name or a label. This should be done patiently, matter-of-factly, and without criticism or undue hysterics. Simply telling the child "Robbie, you look kind of mad" is more useful than asking the child "Robbie, how come you're always going around looking so mad?" The first statement, pointing out that Robbie looks angry, attaches a name to the feeling, helps the child understand it, and encourages him to express it with words. The second question, about why Robbie is always looking so angry, will likely bring back a response that says "I am not, quit picking on me!" It is more important for young children to know *what* they feel, not *why* they feel a certain way.

Teach Creative Communication

Another way to improve communication when dealing with young children is to express the child's wishes for them, when those seem obvious. When five-year-old Erick is furious with three-year-old brother David for getting into his toys, the anger should be acknowledged. However, it may not be enough to accept his statement that "David is a pest!" A simple statement to Erick that "you wish your brother would ask before he took your toys" helps to put the older child's anger into a meaningful context. The problem then is not that David is a "pest" (although he very well might be!) but that David does not ask before taking his brother's toys. This suggests a possible solution for the problem to both Erick and David, and may even encourage some discussion or understanding between them.

Play and Communicate Feelings Other methods for improving communication are to provide a creative outlet for feelings. Young children in particular may not have the words or verbal maturity to express feelings, but they can draw a picture which "shows" how they feel. They may also enjoy playing with toy figures, where the toys represent people they know. In that situation, the parent needs to be careful not to play "therapist" and interpret the child's behavior to them, no matter how tempting that may feel for the parent! Simply playing along and making general comments is enough. Older children may prefer to write a letter to a parent, teacher, or friend, which provides a way to express feelings even if the letters are never given to the person. Finally, a child's feelings must be taken seriously even if they don't make sense to the parent, or the situation is not very serious. A child should never be ridiculed because he or she doesn't like something they're wearing, for example. To them it's a big deal, and in their minds they look pretty terrible and will become the laughingstock of the whole fourth grade. Acknowledging the feeling and providing some support will go a long ways toward making the child feel better. When a child feels understood, and taken seriously, the hurt diminishes and the trust between parent and child grows.

Why Actions Speak Louder Than Words

All children respond better to actions, not words. Most parents, on the other hand, try too hard to talk, explain, persuade, or cajole. As the psychologist Samuel Goldstein Ph.D. put it so succinctly in his advice to parents, "Act, don't yak!" Messages to young children should be kept short, direct, and specific. When parents need to follow through, they should follow through with actions and not with more words or a lecture. Particularly when a child is upset and wants to argue, the parent should resist the temptation to get into an argument or debate and instead respond with a behavioral consequence.

With a young child, ages two to five, who by nature and developmental level is basically selfish and undisciplined, the parent is most effective in a "dictator" role ("I'm your mommy and I said so"). Young children respond to might and authority, not logic. They are motivated by avoiding punishment or earning rewards. Parents make the rules, and they still have all the answers in the child's eyes (that won't last very long!). Parents make decisions about what is fair, and even though the child will argue with this he will usually accept the parents' ruling. It is not necessary and in fact probably confusing to the child to engage in long discussions about *why* something is fair or not fair. When discipline is required, the child may take a time-out, go to his room for isolation, or lose privileges.

Discussion Comes In

By the early grade school years, children develop a larger vocabulary and better verbal comprehension and reasoning skills. It becomes more appropriate to have some discussions about the reasons for having rules and parental requests. The "why" questions will come up more on the child's part. This should not be mistaken for rebelliousness, because often they simply want to know *why* a parent wants a certain thing done. At this point the dictator role needs to give way to something that is more democratic, or at least participatory. Children learn to negotiate and discover that if they give more, they usually get more. Rewards become more effective, even for longer-term projects. The child can project into the future better and plan ahead. After an argument, a cooling-off period should be followed by a discussion about the problem behavior and plans for change.

By the late grade school years, it becomes important to promote more discussion of feelings and thoughts. Rules and responsibilities can be negotiated further. The parents are still in charge of course, but the child develops a greater sense of independence which is natural and healthy. The peer group becomes more influential, although not to the same degree as during the teenage years. Parental authority and rules are still respected as long as they are "fair."

Teen Years: Negotiating Rough Terrain

The teenage years often become the most rocky for the parent-child relationship. At this point, the child's focus of interest shifts in many ways from the parents and family to the peer group. The nice, respectful twelve-year-old becomes a fourteen-year-old and usually begins to challenge the parents more. Even more shocking in the parents' eyes, the teen now finds fault with parental values, behaviors, and rules. Many a couple, faced with the teen son or daughter becoming rebellious, have turned to each other and wondered, "where did we go wrong?"

The answer is, probably, nowhere. The adolescent search for independence is predictable and normal. It cannot be "prevented," but it should be managed as well as can be. This period is when the parents must remain strong and not buckle under to pressure. For all their striving for independence, adolescents still need a sense of belonging and being rooted in their families. Teens should be held accountable for their behavior, at home, at school, and in society. With increased freedoms and privileges come increased responsibility and accountability.

Rules for Teens   Rules and responsibilities for teens can be discussed and negotiated to some degree, with the crucial exception of the important rules affecting health, safety, and avoiding legal problems, which the parents must make non-negotiable. Curfews need to be enforced, for example, and are not subject to negotiation except under very special conditions. Parents must have the last word on important matters. As much as the teens may grumble, if the parents hold firm, the teens will eventually comply. The consequences for breaking important rules should have enough bite to them to be meaningful for the teen. Parents must, must, must be consistent in enforcing rules, otherwise the rules lose meaning and the parents lose authority. When it doesn't involve risks to their health or safety, or have very serious long-term consequences such as failing school or having a criminal record, teens can benefit the most from being allowed to suffer the natural consequences of their behavior. Protecting them and rescuing them from their irresponsible behavior does little to train the teens for becoming truly independent and self-sufficient in the real world.

Choose Your Communication Style

Communicating with your children on the child's level is something most people learn on the fly. Some things parents communicate are important at any age or level of development. Starting from infancy, parents can communicate a patient, understanding, and loving attitude. They can also communicate a distant and uncaring attitude toward their children which produces deep wounds and often turns minor problems and conflicts into major ones. Even worse, parents can communicate a critical, demeaning, shaming attitude which becomes truly abusive. Any communication between parent and child should protect the integrity of the child, along with their often fragile self-esteem and still developing sense of identity.

Chapter **5**

"We'll See Who Can Yell the Loudest"

P ower struggles between parent and child are common. They start from the time a toddler begins to crawl around and explore her brave new world. The limits on the child's behavior begin: don't touch the stove, don't pull the dog's tail, put away your toys, do your homework, put on your pajamas, and so on. None of us like too many limits placed on our behavior, even if it *is* for our own good! The nature of the power struggles changes and evolves somewhat with the age of the child, but continues in some form until the children grow up and leave home.

DON'T SET UP POWER STRUGGLES

Power struggles can be frustrating and emotionally draining. They often result in angry confrontations if parent and child butt heads. They cannot be totally avoided, but prevented at times if the parent uses some foresight and planning. When power struggles develop, as they certainly will, the trick is to defuse the anger and resolve the situation as quickly and painlessly as possible.

Independence Is Healthy

Power struggles often get worse around the times when children are establishing their sense of independence. This can vary with age and maturity level, but the themes tend to be consistent. A two-year-old child, going through the familiar stage of the "terrible twos," is literally establishing physical independence from the parent, as well as exploring the world. The child discovers the freedom to move around, make decisions, express feelings through physical behavior, and most of all that she is an independent being from the other people around her. The children lack the maturity to make important decisions of course, or to avoid the dangers in the world around them, consequently the parents develop structure, plans, and discipline. This will not be the last time the child experiences deep frustration over the perceived ability to make choices, but also the lack of freedom to make those choices.

Adolescence brings about a different set of problems and conflicts for children and parents, centered around the need of the child to achieve psychological independence. During these often turbulent times, the search for independence and identity provides a battleground over rules, limits, freedoms, responsibilities, and privileges. To say that this struggle is normal does not make it any less stressful or frustrating. The types of dangers also get more complicated and serious, including drinking, drugs, sex and pregnancy, and delinquent behavior. Just when the teenager seeks more independence, the parent sees more dangers to worry about and a need for firmer controls. No wonder that disagreements and conflicts develop, and sparks fly emotionally. How conflictual this period becomes does not depend simply on how compliant or rebellious the adolescent is, but also is very much related to how the parents handle these issues of independence. Parents are seldom as helpless as they might feel, however they need to assert themselves in constructive ways and prevent conflicts rather than contribute to them or make them worse.

Why Kids and Parents Get Into Power Struggles

Your children won't always agree with you, and you won't always agree with them. Dissension, disagreement, and conflict are part of normal life. At times, conflicts arise not because of some huge disagreement over rules or principles, but simply because the child is having a bad day. Some days it just seems like nothing is good enough, and nothing will please them, no matter how hard you try. Those periods of negativity will try your patience to the utmost. As Dr. Edward Hallowell points out in his book *When You Worry About The Child You Love,* kids (and adults) have aggression built into them as part of our human biological condition. Frustration and disappointment can easily turn to anger, and develop into a conflict. The question for you, mom or dad, is not *if* conflicts will develop but rather *how* you will respond when they do develop.

A Logic All Their Own   Adults respond to problems and conflicts in life in a logical and rational manner, or at least we like to think that we behave that way! Children on the other hand often behave emotionally, not rationally. They can be extremely stubborn, resist all logic, and overreact emotionally to a situation. This can be very frustrating and confusing to many parents who wonder why the child does not understand or respect the logic of the parents' rule or request. The child *knows* that homework must be done, and *knows* that the rule is to do an hour of study time after dinner. Why then will the kid put up such a fuss about sitting down and starting their homework? "She is trying to get my goat," the parent might conclude, or "he likes to get into these arguments with me." It helps to keep such behavior in perspective and not overreact to it.

Don't You Act Like a Child   When a child behaves in a manner that makes no logical sense because "he knows better," or blows up over "nothing," that child may simply be acting like a child. The wise parent will expect the immature, emotional behavior and deal with it as best as can be done under the circumstances. It never helps to take the child's protesting too seriously, regard it as a personal attack, or overreact to it. Taking the child's obnoxious behavior personally, overreacting emotionally, and getting into an argument about it would make the parent act like, well, a child. Consider what usually happens when two children fight.

How Parents Make It Worse

It's a safe bet to say that at times our children will do things that frustrate us and make us angry. When *we,* as adults and parents, overreact to the children's behavior and engage in a battle with them, it makes them even more emotional and less cooperative. This is when power struggles develop. The parent or other adult who tries to bully a child into submission with a heads-on battle is asking for it—you might as well wave a red flag in front of a charging bull. As Drs. Silberman and Wheelan make clear in *How to Discipline Without Feeling Guilty,* "there is nothing that increases strong-willed children's adrenaline more than when adults entice them into battle." There is nothing that will bring on a power struggle quicker than when the parent loses his or her cool and tries to become the controlling authoritarian.

When parents get into arguments with their child, the power struggles follow. Indeed, arguments are power struggles that nobody wins. Has any parent ever won an argument with a five-year-old? The child can be coerced into doing what the parent wants, but that does not mean the child agrees with the parents' thinking, thinks the parent is acting fairly, or feels understood and appreciated. Enforcing a rule calmly but firmly is not the same thing as yelling at a child and criticizing them for not doing what you want, which is what an argument comes down to. Children have a need to maintain pride and dignity as much as adults, even very young children. Getting yelled at and being criticized hurts their pride, sense of dignity, and willingness to cooperate in the long run. What the child may walk away with is the feeling that "I'm always getting yelled at," and perhaps "nobody cares about me," with some "I'll show you" likely thrown in for future consideration. The child gets the sense of being punished, rather than of the parent acting in the child's best interest. It certainly does not *feel* like somebody has your interests at heart when they are yelling at you. There are only losers in an argument, no winners.

Don't Give In Another way that parents can make the power struggles worse is to give in to the child. The parent who has not yet learned how to say no, and mean it, will find himself in a battle with the child for the simple reason that the child learns that arguing works! If children find they can push you into giving in to their demands, they will test you at every turn. Don't give in if you are making a decision that is best for the child, or enforcing a rule that has been agreed to, even if the child makes a scene about it. Don't let them off the hook! It is never in the child's best interest to let them bully you or pressure you into going against your best judgment. The parent who is inconsistent and allows the child to bully them "only" once in a while is asking for a protracted battle also. What the child is learning from the parents' inconsistent behavior is that bullying, pressure, or making a scene *might work,* and that will be enough to make a heated conflict worthwhile for the child. Children can be incredibly persistent if there is a chance they will get what they want, as all parents learn at some point.

CARLY AND HER MOM

Carly is ten years old. It is Saturday morning, and she is in the kitchen talking excitedly on the phone with her friend Susan when her mother walks into the room.

"Carly, time to clean your room," her mother tells her politely.

The girl is clearly annoyed with this demand on her time and makes a face. "No, I'm talking to Susan about her party tomorrow!" she replies in an irritated tone.

Carly's mother is surprised at her daughter's defiance and gives her a stern look. "Don't you talk back to me, young lady. I told you to clean your room, now do it! The rule is that you clean your room on Saturday mornings, or did you forget?"

"No!" Carly shouts. "I'm talking to Susan and the room looks just fine!"

The mother gives her a stern look, hands set on her hips. This is a universal fighting stance. "I said do it right now, or you're grounded off the phone for the day. It's your choice."

"I'll do it later" Carly whines and rolls her eyes. Her mom is such a nag!

"That's it, you're grounded from the phone for the day. I want you to get off the phone now and clean your room. I said now! When I tell you to do something, I expect you to do it and not argue with me!"

"Mom, you are such a nag! I'm just talking to Susan about her party! I'm not going to clean the stupid room, it's clean already!"

"All right Carly, you're grounded off the phone for a week," her mother fumes. "Want to try for two weeks?"

Carly jumps up from her chair and glares at her mother, her face getting red. "I'm not cleaning it and you can't make me!" she shouts. "This is a free country and it's my room! Now get off my back!"

"That's it, you're grounded off the phone for two weeks. Shall we try for a month?"

"This is so unfair!" Carly protests. "None of my friend's parents are as mean as you!"

"I do more for you than a lot of your friends' parents, and you know it. I really resent hearing that from you!" the mother exclaims, feeling hurt and getting even angrier with her daughter. "Now go clean your room or you're not going to Susan's birthday party tomorrow. I mean it!"

"You can't do that," Carly protests, a little in shock. Susan is her best friend.

"Oh, can't I? Just watch me," her mother threatens. "Now for the last time, are you going to go and clean your room or not?"

Carly raises the phone over her head, as if to throw it, then catches herself just in time and slams it on the kitchen table instead. "I hate you!" she screams, tears rolling down her cheeks.

"Fine, I'll clean the room if that will make you so happy! I hate living in this house!"

"Oh great, now you hate me!" her mother shouts after Carly, who storms into her room and slams the door shut.

Dousing Flames Takes Water, Not Gasoline

The escalation in tension and conflict between Carly and her mother was equally upsetting for both of them. The argument left both feeling furious, hurt, and resentful. Carly finally cleaned her room, but at a huge emotional price for both daughter and mother. This scenario illustrates how a direct battle of wills can quickly escalate into a heated battle, with tempers flaring and anger threatening to become physical. If the argument becomes heated enough, children may swear or call the parent names, destroy property, or even hit the parent. If parents lose it, they may become abusive and resort to hitting as well.

Now consider a different scenario between Carly and her mother, where the conflict is handled more calmly and does not escalate:

"Carly, time to clean your room," her mother tells her politely.

"No, I'm talking to Susan about her party tomorrow!" Carly replies in an irritated tone.

"Carly, you know the rule, you clean your room every Saturday morning. It's now 10 o'clock, I want your room cleaned by noon or else you're grounded," her mother replies firmly but pleasantly.

"But I'm talking to Susan and the room looks clean to me, for goodness sakes!" Carly protests.

"I want it cleaned by noon, or you're grounded until it gets cleaned," her mother replies. "That means if it's not cleaned by tomorrow, you're also grounded tomorrow." The mother turns and goes back to the family room.

"Mom, that's not fair!" Carly yells. "Oh, great! Susan, can you believe how unfair my mom is? No, my mom is worse, really! Look,

I have to go, mom says I have to clean my room or else I'm grounded. This is so annoying! I'll call you later, okay?"

How to Prevent Getting into a Power Struggle

Since power struggles cannot be entirely avoided, the best bet for parents is to try to anticipate problems or conflicts that may arise, and how to cope with them. When the conflict comes you want to have a plan in place, keep your wits about you, and enforce the rules assertively but calmly. If you become angry and lose it emotionally, so will your child. That leads to argument and escalation of conflict.

One of the keys to avoiding or minimizing power struggles is to be very clear with your children about what is expected of them. Although this may sound like an obvious point, its importance cannot be overstated. Indeed, it is such a basic principle that many parents take it for granted and give it short shrift. Children need structure and consistent rules. If there are no consistent rules, as Dr. Hallowell describes in *When You Worry About the Child You Love,* they make up their own. The rules need to be discussed so that they are clearly understood. They don't have to be the same for every child, but may be different for each child depending on his developmental level and the behaviors or responsibilities the parents wish to emphasize. It may be helpful to have a family negotiation session to discuss what the rules of the house are. The rules can be written down as a contract, signed by each family member, and posted where they can be seen by all. The door or side of the refrigerator is a favorite place for many families to post the rules. The rules should be reviewed and discussed as frequently as necessary. Young children in particular get distracted by many things, and will need gentle reminders of exactly what the rules are.

Set Up Clear and Fair Rules   There should not be too many or it gets confusing. A handful of important rules work much better than a long list of both the crucial and the mundane. Simple rules enforced consistently are understood and internalized by even very young children. Tell them what is expected of them when a friend comes over to play, for example, anticipating what some of the problems might be and letting the child know how you want them to behave. Establish simple responsibilities around set routines, such as putting away toys before watching TV. Monitor and supervise the child's behavior as needed. Getting into a habit of cooperatively discussing and enforcing rules sets the stage for greater trust and cooperation as the children get older.

Rules need to be enforceable, of course. Never fight a battle you can't win, and never set a rule you can't enforce. Plan ahead about what to do when the rules are broken, as some of them most certainly will be. What will you do if your child breaks curfew? Calls you an obscene name? Comes home intoxicated from a party? Skips school? It helps to have a general plan in mind, then enforce the rules as promised.

Positive behaviors need to be encouraged, just as much as negative behaviors need to be discouraged. The wise parent uses rewards and praise as well as punishments and negative consequences. Praise the child for acting responsibly, being helpful and cooperative, and handling disputes in a calm and fair manner.

Some children lack the social skills or emotional maturity to know how to communicate their disagreements without getting into an argument or conflict. In those situations, the constructive solution is to teach them more helpful communication skills, not to criticize or punish bad behavior. Young children in particular need to be taught acceptable ways to resolve differences and disagreements without conflict. It is better to take turns when playing a video game, for example, rather than fighting over the game controller. Similarly, it is expected that children will ask parents for permission before going outside or taking food from the refrigerator. These set routines can help a great deal to reduce the likelihood of conflicts with peers, siblings, parents, and other adults.

Finally, parents should always keep in mind that they are role models. If you use anger and aggression in handling your conflicts and disputes, so will your children. They learn from watching you interact with them, as well as with other people. What are they learning from your behavior and the way you handle conflicts? What do you wish to teach them?

The Power Paradox

"Winning" a power struggle with your child does not imply out-shouting them or bullying them, but rather keeping your cool. As we've discussed in this chapter, getting too emotional, arguing, or trying to control the child's behavior makes the power struggles worse, not better. The most influential person is not the one who shouts the loudest, but the one whose voice carries the most weight. Clearly that person is and should be the parent. Finally, the best way to "win" a power struggle with a child is to avoid having one in the first place. This can be accomplished in part by anticipating problems and conflicts, and having strategies in place for how to deal with them. Sometimes the best solution for a conflict or argument is to state your position and walk away from it. The value of winning an argument is overrated, and the battle itself, win or lose, is seldom worth the grief it can cause.

If conflicts between children and parents become chronic or simply too angry and heated, they may require professional help. Some children who argue with their parents excessively or seem angry a lot may be displacing their frustrations related to problems with friends, school, or another family member. This may also be an indication of an emotional problem, such as childhood depression. It is important to be sensitive to the causes of their anger and repeated tendency to get into conflicts with others. Similarly, if the child is physically hurting himself, hurting others, or destroying property, it would be a good time to consult a mental health professional. Finally, if a parent loses control and becomes verbally or physically abusive, it is imperative that he or she get help. Family therapy as well as individual therapy can provide crucial benefits when conflicts get out of control.

Chapter **6**

Deal with Anger Constructively

> "I was angry with my friend: I told my wrath and my wrath did end.
>
> I was angry with my foe: I told it not, my wrath did grow."
>
> —WILLIAM BLAKE, "A Poison Tree"

A nger is one of the most basic, natural, common feelings human beings experience. The ways in which we express anger may change at different periods in our lives, but we never stop feeling it or expressing it. Infants cry, young children whine, teenagers sulk or rebel, adults argue or become passive aggressive, and the elderly become irritable and cantankerous.

DON'T CENSOR OR PUNISH ANGRY FEELINGS

Children in particular are not mature enough to deal with anger well and must be taught to express it in appropriate ways. Angry teens are more prone to acting out in destructive ways such as fighting, lying, delinquent behavior, skipping school, and drug abuse. The children with anger control problems who don't learn how to deal with it constructively will become adults with anger problems who ruin relationships, lose jobs, develop high blood pressure or heart problems, or get themselves thrown in jail.

Accepting Anger

Anger is here to stay. The challenges for parents is how to best teach their children to recognize it, accept it, and manage it so that their anger causes the fewest disruptions in daily living and the least strain on family relationships. The parenting challenges are somewhat different at different stages in their child's development. The goal with young children may be simply to help them recognize anger and express it appropriately. "Appropriate" usually means verbally, or some symbolic expression of anger which does not cause harm and is not abusive. The goal with teens may be more pragmatic, to set rules and limits, enforce them, and avoid endless battles around arguments and nagging.

Expressing Anger

Young kids need to have their feelings acknowledged, and be taught how to put them into words. This is particularly true with feelings of anger. If verbal expression of anger is denied, chances are the anger will come out in their behavior in some way. Children who are not allowed to be angry, or are punished for it, may even develop physiological reactions such as more frequent headaches, stomachaches, and appetite or sleep problems. Most young children are naturally aggressive and impulsive, thus one of the key lessons is to "Say it with words!" Although the angry words and emotional expression may sound terrible, it's better than physical violence. Talking about what makes us angry, "getting it off your chest" usually helps us vent some of the feelings and calm down.

When verbal expression is not a good option, for example because the object of the child's anger is not around or because the child is too young and has a limited vocabulary, some kind of symbolic expression of the anger can be just as useful. Writing a letter can do wonders to give the anger symbolic expression, for example to a teacher or an absent parent. The letter is usually best not sent, but it serves its purpose nonetheless for the person writing it. Even very young children can be asked to "draw me a picture to show me how mad you are." Very young children may be encouraged to show their anger in playing with their dolls, while the parent watches and makes some comments acknowledging, identifying, and thus validating the child's feelings.

The Parent's Attitude

Angry feelings should not be dismissed, ridiculed, or punished. The parental admonition to an angry child that "you shouldn't feel that way" will probably just further frustrate and anger the child who obviously *does* feel that way. How much better it is to acknowledge and validate the child's feelings of anger. If Sara gets furious because Linda took her dollhouse from her room, and starts screaming "I hate you Sara!" to her sister, the parent can react in different ways that will shape how Linda and Sara deal with anger. If the parent feels uncomfortable with the child's anger and tells Linda that "you don't really hate your sister" or that "you shouldn't hate your sister" or even that "in this family we don't hate each other," what is the message for Linda?

What Linda (and probably Sara too) might learn from that statement is that it's not okay to be honest about feelings, not okay to feel angry, and even possibly that feeling real angry toward someone in the family makes you a bad person! A more helpful response might be to acknowledge Linda's feelings and the reason for them. If the parent responds with a statement such as "I can see that it makes you very angry when Sara takes your things without asking first," it communicates to Linda that she is being heard and that her feelings of anger are okay. The statement further connects the anger to a cause. It communicates a possible solution to both Linda and Sara, namely that you better ask first before you take your sister's belongings or it causes bad feelings. Having Sara help to carry the dollhouse back into Linda's room would make that message even clearer to both girls.

Angry Feelings, Angry Acts

Dr. Haim Ginott, in his classic book *Between Parent and Child*, pointed out that children should be taught the important difference

between angry feelings and angry acts. Feelings need to be identified and expressed. Again, if angry feelings are forbidden or punished they will find other outlets and cause other problems. Angry
acts on the other hand have to be limited or at times redirected. It's
okay to feel angry with your brother, for example, but it's *not* okay
to hit him! Parents must set the limits on behavior, and then
enforce them. Limits can be set as early as six months of age, for
example not allowing hitting or throwing things in anger. The limits should be explained clearly to the child, as many times as necessary, and then enforced consistently. Consequences for physically
aggressive behavior need to be immediate and have some impact
on the child's freedoms, privileges, or access to goodies. Some rules
are universally helpful and should be implemented from an early
age. "No hitting" is a pretty good rule to follow for every family
member—children and adults. "No name calling" helps to avoid
arguments and fights. "No nagging" is generally a wise rule for parents who wish to avoid their children getting angry with them and
precipitating an argument.

Look for Cues and Clues   Children (and adults!) can be taught how to
recognize the cues of getting angry, and thus develop better anger
control by catching themselves sooner in the anger cycle. Muscle
tension in the jaw, neck, hands, or chest are typical early physiological signs of anger coming on. Cognitive messages can also be early
warning signals, such as "she's being so unfair" or "that's it, I've had
it." The person can learn to identify these signals and take some
action to defuse the anger. Walking away from a tense situation
usually helps. Particularly in a family conflict, when a person needs
to walk away and cool off they should be allowed to do so. Don't
chase after them unless you want to escalate the conflict! Very little
communication takes place when someone is truly angry, except
the message of "I am angry!" Better to let tempers cool off first and
then have a discussion.

Dealing with Anger Constructively

If you find yourself feeling very angry, there are things that will help tone it down. Talk more slowly and softer—truly angry people talk fast and loud. If you're standing, sit down. A person sitting looks less threatening to others, and also may feel less agitated. Get a drink of water (not alcohol or caffeine) to help you cool down. Keep your hands and feet to your sides and try to be still. It does not help at all to look or act physically threatening, since that makes others around you get into a battle mentality. Tell yourself mentally to "calm down" or "shut up." No one wins an argument, not even parents. No child has ever been "argued" into good behavior. It is much more constructive, and less stressful, to have clear rules, which are communicated and enforced consistently, than to get involved in heated arguments with your child.

The Rage of Angels   If a child becomes so angry that he or she goes into a rage, the first order of business for the parents is to keep their own anger in check. Keep in mind that anger feeds on anger, and the last thing an angry child who may feel out of control needs to see is the parent or parents also losing control. The second order of business is to remove the child from the angry situation and to a low-stress environment. It helps to use short sentences and speak soothingly. This is not the time for criticisms, and certainly not the time for lectures on how the child ought to behave or how when you were a kid your parents never tolerated this kind of behavior. It is usually not a good idea to put your hands on a child who is in an angry rage, as he or she may retaliate physically by hitting, kicking, biting, and so on. The exception would be if the parent-child relationship is such that the parent knows touching will soothe the child and help him calm down.

Anger and Teens   Whereas the goal for helping young children deal with anger is to acknowledge it and help them express it in healthy ways, the goal with teenage children may be to basically keep the anger in check. One of the cardinal rules for parents of teens, as Thomas Phelan makes clear in his book *Surviving Your Adolescents,* is simply this: don't argue! Arguing only strengthens the battle lines between parent and child. Not arguing with your teenagers doesn't mean that you let them have their way to do whatever they choose, of course. Parents must still assert their parental authority, set rules, and enforce them. Negotiations and give and take are necessary at times, much more so than when children are little. This is not capitulation or weakness on the part of the parents, but rather acceptance of the teenager's needs to establish some sense of independence and to start making more of their own decisions in life. The controlling parents who cannot allow the child to mature and grow independent will be more likely to have an angry, battling adolescent on their hands. If the problems become chronic or severe, it may require an objective evaluation and suggestions for change from a professional.

Some Causes of Anger

What causes children to get angry in the family environment? Many a beleaguered parent would say, "everything!" Young children respond to not getting what they want, when they want it. It can become extremely annoying to listen to a young child's incessant demands, but that's part of the territory. Their right to ask for things should be acknowledged, as well as the parent's right to set limits and say "no." As children get older, their perception of unfairness becomes more acute. Woe be unto the parent who treats their child unfairly, often in comparison to a sibling or a friend. Instances of siblings "borrowing" things without permission are common and usually generate an angry response. Infringements of privacy ("snooping") by the parents can cause strong feelings of resentment and anger. This is sometimes a legitimate gripe that children have if the parents are overcontrolling and don't allow their children much privacy. Being teased about things they don't feel good about can quickly produce resentment and anger. Being talked about by others in negative ways is something that all children dread and react to by becoming upset.

Sorting Out the Source   Parents should keep in mind that many times the anger their child directs at them may not involve the parent directly. The child may be upset with an incident at school for example, and the parent catches the brunt of the child's anger over some trivial issue at home. Is the child really upset over meatloaf being served for dinner for the second week in a row, or is he upset about the bully who picked on him in gym class? If he's embarrassed to talk about the bully, his anger may come out in his passionate dislike for meatloaf and lack of variety in mom's meal planning! Kids in early adolescence are often hesitant to express their anger toward their peers, and consequently parents or siblings catch it instead. Family members, particularly siblings, make safer targets for the child's anger than do peers, teachers, or other adults who make them angry.

The "safest" target for anger in many families is of course good old mom. Mothers tend to be more tolerant, understanding, and nurturing, and less likely to retaliate or reject the person who becomes angry with them. Not only do most mothers deserve a medal for that, but unfortunately they also catch the brunt of severe anger and defiant behaviors when children develop emotional or behavioral problems. It is important for mothers in particular to gage how much "flak" they are getting on a regular basis, and if it's too much, to assert themselves and not accept any abuse. If need be, help should be called in, from a spouse, other adults in the family, or a professional who works with behavioral problems.

Setting an Example

One of the best things parents can do for their children, in terms of teaching them how to deal with anger, is to model good behavior for them. Does the parent allow himself or herself to show anger in healthy ways? Do the parents show restraint in not becoming destructive or abusive? Do they refrain from calling people names or criticizing? Do they resist being drawn into arguments, and do they stop arguments effectively once they start? Do the parents hit or throw things? Hitting is never a good idea, even in the guise of spanking young children. Hitting gives the child the message that "when you're angry—hit!" Parents who spank need to learn better ways of setting and enforcing limits. Most important, we as parents need to behave in responsible ways if we expect our children to act responsibly. Children are wonderful learning machines, and they learn a great deal from watching us. What kinds of role models will we provide?

Chapter **7**

Discipline with Love, Not Abuse

Good discipline is healthy. As much as children may complain about it (and they will!), discipline is a method to teach right from wrong, to motivate, and to keep order in the family. All children need to learn to become responsible, considerate, and respectful in the ways they relate to people in their lives. They need to learn to make good decisions and to avoid things that can get them into trouble, or that are outright dangerous. Loving, effective discipline can provide all these things for our children and more.

DON'T USE DISCIPLINE AS PUNISHMENT

What makes a problem a major problem, and how should a parent respond? Some problems are clearly serious, such as drug abuse, crime, or abusive behavior. In *Surviving Your Adolescents*, psychologist Thomas Phelan describes a system for parents to classify behaviors according to degree of seriousness and damage the behaviors can cause. He calls this the "major/moderate/minor" system.

Keeping Things in Perspective

"Major" offenses require swift and meaningful action. Examples might include drinking and driving, staying out all night without permission, shoplifting, and physical violence. Consequences might include being grounded to the house for two weeks, losing phone or car privileges for a month, or a hefty cash fine which the teen will have to pay or work off for the parents by doing ten hours of extra chores around the house. A "medium" offense includes things such as smoking cigarettes before the age of sixteen, using profanity toward the parents, or getting into behavioral trouble at school. Consequences might be half as severe compared to major offenses, for example no phone for two weeks or doing five hours of extra chores. "Minor" offenses include things such as leaving the house unlocked, or lying about doing chores. Consequences might include no phone for three days, or doing three hours of extra chores.

It is important for the parents to have a general picture of how to respond to these types of problems. Some things are clearly off limits, and these should be discussed and made clear to the child or teen. Drug use is not acceptable, for example, or shoplifting, or physical violence. If these rules are broken, then consequences must be enforced swiftly and consistently, without argument or negotiating. In situations where drug use, school failure, unwanted pregnancy, or another health problem is involved, the parents reactions may need to include getting help as opposed to simply disciplining behavior.

Healthy and Unhealthy Discipline

Healthy discipline is very much a teaching tool. It teaches good behavior, sets good examples, and expresses mutual love and respect between the parent and child. Children learn best when they love us, not when they're afraid of us or punished every time they step out of line. Healthy discipline is never based on criticism or punishments. Unhealthy discipline, unfortunately, is based mostly on punishments as a way to "correct" behavior. Many parents in fact equate the very notion of discipline with punishment. When they say that "he deserves to be disciplined," what they really mean is "he deserves a good beating!" This is sad, destructive, and doomed to fail. Good behavior cannot be "beaten into" anyone, and the parents who rely on punishments are not going to be affective parents.

Discipline as Punishment

Psychologists have known for a long time that relying on punishment as the major means of discipline is horrendously bad for both the child and parent. We know that rewarding good behavior changes behavior over time so that it's more likely to be repeated. Reward a child for putting away dirty plates and glasses, with verbal praise and a hug for example, and after some time the child is likely to get into a habit of putting away his or her dirty plates and glasses.

On the other hand, we know that punishing bad behavior does not really change the long-term behavior. Rather, punishment suppresses behavior temporarily when the punishment is in effect. Punish a child for watching cartoons on TV, and the child won't watch cartoons on TV *when the parent is home*! When bad behavior is punished, it does not necessarily go away. Many times the child simply learns to hide it better to escape punishments. Punishments that are painful and degrading are often emotionally traumatic. What these teach the person is that she is a "bad" person, and they play havoc with the child's self-esteem and basic sense of worth. This is toxic, destructive discipline.

When Children Fight Back

It is very common to see children who are disciplined with punishments eventually fight back. Parents who discipline their children through verbal or physical aggression do a good job mostly of teaching their children how to be aggressive. What the child learns is that "might makes right," and that if you want someone to do what you want them to do, you yell at them, threaten them, or hit them. Often, as the children get older, the aggression is turned back against the parents who then cry that "my child is out of control!"

Many children who are punished excessively will try to punish the parents back by not doing what the parents want. They adopt a defiant, "I'll show you" attitude that sets up an ongoing power struggle where everybody loses. Dr. Bruno Bettelheim tells a story about a young boy who became so angry he stopped talking altogether and thus stopped functioning in his everyday life. In discussing the problem with a therapist, it came out that the boy was angry about having his mouth washed out with soap when he said bad words. His angry "I'll show you" response to his parents behavior was that "if you wash out the bad words with soap, you wash out the good words too, and I won't have any words to say anymore." This young child fought back against harsh, abusive discipline in the only way that he knew, by withholding something his parents wanted, even though his behavior hurt himself more.

When Discipline Becomes Abuse

Discipline can become abusive even when parents have good intentions. Most parents care about their children and want the best for them, even those who use punishments excessively. Often these parents worry about their children's future. They punish as a result of their own anxiety and worry, not because the child's behavior deserves the punishment. Sometimes the parents were punished or abused themselves when they were growing up, and are modeling the abusive behavior of their own parents because they don't know any better. In either case, using punishments excessively is not healthy, does not lead to good methods of discipline, and does not provide good parenting.

Parents can learn better parenting skills of course, but sadly they often don't even realize the harm they are causing. Sometimes reading a book such as this one helps to increase awareness. Often it becomes necessary for abusive parents to work with a child therapist to learn better parenting skills, and/or join a support group for abusive parents. If there is abuse going on, whether it be emotional, physical, or sexual, the abusive parent can (and should) lose custody rights over the child. Dangerous, sick parents who commit sexual abuse or serious physical abuse can be prosecuted and can end up in jail or prison. Thankfully, most parents are not abusive.

Effective Discipline

Healthy and effective discipline involves many things, and good parents use many of the skills naturally. Good discipline involves protecting the child's self-esteem and sense of integrity, teaching responsible behaviors, and building an atmosphere of cooperation, trust, love, and respect. Effective discipline focuses on behavior, never on the child's character or worth. If discipline requires some reasonable punishment (for example, you kicked the dog therefore you lose TV privileges for a day), the focus should be on punishing the bad behavior, not the "bad" child. The distinction should be made for the child very clearly.

Some rules of thumb to keep in mind which make for humane, effective discipline:

Good Discipline

- wait until a child is calm and in control before attempting to discuss the situation
- stay calm, don't get hysterical, and never argue with your child
- focus on behavior, don't threaten self-esteem
- deal with one thing at a time

- be in charge when using discipline, don't be meek or ask the child's permission
- use immediate consequences when possible, particularly with young children
- make the punishment fit the crime
- use consequences that are meaningful for that child and make an impact

- be brief; no long lectures allowed!
- use positives before negatives, try rewarding good behavior
- describe the problem behavior and discuss alternative behavior
- use natural consequences when possible; the rule is "if you abuse it, you lose it"
- try to anticipate problems and have a plan, for example when your teen starts to drive
- don't take the child's misbehavior personally and overreact to it

Common Errors in Discipline

Bad approaches to discipline usually damage the child's self-esteem, set up a "me against you" atmosphere, discourage cooperation and trust, and reduce a child's sense of being in control or being able to behave responsibly. As we discussed above, relying on frequent or excessive punishments is a sure way to cause damage to your relationship with your child, and to lose effectiveness as a parent.

Some rules of thumb to keep in mind for what leads to ineffective discipline:

Bad Discipline

- discipline that is inappropriate for child's developmental age
- inconsistency in applying consequences
- arguing
- threatening
- bargaining
- sarcasm
- lectures
- indirect or unclear messages
- accepting promises
- disagreements and disunity between parents
- getting too emotional
- repeating yourself endlessly
- using guilt
- withdrawing love
- bringing up old sins when angry
- shaming
- using sarcastic and cruel "humor"
- comparison with others

The Virtue of Patience

Good parenting requires patience. This is particularly true when parents need to apply discipline, and more so when disciplining young children. Children need many lessons before behavior is learned or changed, and this may require a great deal of both patience and love. Don't lose patience with your young children! Think about how long it took *you* to learn self-control. Unfortunately, patience is a difficult thing for parents to practice in our hurried culture, and difficult to keep in mind when you're saying "how many times have I told you to _____" (fill in the blank) for the twentieth time.

The wise parent should always keep in mind that it takes many repeated lessons and uses of discipline to teach values and responsible behavior, until the child internalizes the behavior and makes it part of his or her own belief system, outlook on life, and behavioral habits. Some things may require one lesson or reminder, others ten, and others a hundred. It takes as many lessons as it takes.

When Not to Discipline

Even "bad" behavior that is normal for a child's developmental age should not be disciplined. It is not realistic to expect a five-year-old child to stay out of a box of cookies that is left on the kitchen table, for example. It would be more practical and realistic for the parent to place the box of cookies on a high shelf or other location where the child does not have easy access to it. Punishing the behavior won't speed up the child's development of self-control, but will most likely make him feel like a "bad" child who has lost his parent's approval. All children lie occasionally, sometimes because they are playing or fantasizing. The lying behavior might be discussed as being appropriate or not appropriate, but play behavior that is harmless in itself should not be disciplined.

If a child misbehaves but shows a high level of remorse or guilt about it, it may be sufficient to simply discuss and admonish the behavior, then let it go. When children reach preadolescence or early adolescence and begin to assert their independence, it's important for the parent to set priorities and limits, and enforce the ones that are deemed nonnegotiable. If a parent reacts to every challenge of rule or authority by their teenager with discipline or punishment, life in the family will soon resemble a daily war zone! Choose your battles wisely, and let minor things slide.

The Power of Modeling

Our children model our behavior. This can be good news or bad news, depending, of course, on *us* and what types of examples we set for them. The good news is that the more they love and respect us, the more likely they are to imitate and copy our values and behaviors. Parents who model good behaviors for their children actually need to use *less* discipline with their children. Ask yourself who is likely to listen and learn better: a child who loves his parents, feels loved by them, and looks up to them? Or a child who fears his parents and feels rejected by them? Clearly the child will emulate the person he or she respects, trusts, and loves more.

Modeling versus Discipline   The parents who are critical, punitive, or hypocritical will have a need to use discipline more often but will also find that the discipline they use is less effective. Most children have a wonderful built-in sensor for hypocrisy and fake behavior. The parents who expect one thing from their children, but do another themselves, have little credibility with their children and little respect. These parents discover that they are also poor at using discipline or getting compliance from their kids. By and large, the parents who model poor behaviors are ineffective parents. Which category of parent do you want to belong to, moms and dads? Your answer, and even more crucially your behavior, will go a long way toward determining how effective you are in providing discipline for your children, and in general how effective you are as a parent.

Chapter **8**

Too Much, Too Soon

U ntil approximately thirty years ago, with the advent of the 1970s decade, most children spent their time around the house or playing with friends and siblings within distance of a bike ride. Many women were at-home moms, and kids spent the preschool years at home being raised by their mothers. The father usually took the one family car to work so there was no opportunity to drive the kids all over town. Life was slower paced, and neighborhood based.

DON'T RUSH CHILDREN INTO GROWING UP

It's tougher being a kid these days. Not only that, but for many children there is simply no time for it! Children get signed up for recreational activities from the time they're in nursery school. Millions of mothers (sometimes fathers, but most commonly moms) have become personal taxi services for their children, providing transportation from soccer practice to tutor to sister's ballet lesson to Bobby's birthday party at the recreation center, along with a side trip to pick up some milk at the grocery store. Frequently this happens after mom gets home from her job, or during her "free" time on weekends. There is little opportunity for parent and child to work on a fun project, have a long chat, or simply spend time relaxing and doing nothing. By the end of the day both child and parents are tired and frazzled. The next morning brings a similar routine.

No Time to Be a Kid

Researchers at the University of Michigan conducted a study in 1997 to see how children twelve and younger spent their time. The findings in this study were, in a nutshell, that kids are busier than ever. Leisure time for children (defined as time left over during the day after sleeping, eating, attending school or day care, and taking care of personal hygiene) has declined from 40 percent of the child's day in 1981 to 25 percent of their day in 1997. Involvement in sports rose 50 percent from 1981 to 1997, with boys spending twice as much time as girls in organized sports activities. Television is not the villain here, because children spent 25 percent *less* time watching TV in 1997 as compared with 1981. The children spent an hour or less a week reading. Children's lives have simply gotten busier.

Common sense tells us that children and families need some structure and organized activities to get things done. Problems arise, however, when the pendulum swings too far in the opposite direction and there is no time to relax, unwind, and simply be together as a family. Kids complain of being bored at times, but they also complain more and more of too many planned activities and obligations. Monday is baseball practice, Tuesday is piano lessons, Wednesday is play practice at school, Thursday is the math tutor and dentist appointment, and Friday is the baseball game, followed by Saturday play practice and swimming lessons. Add homework and some routine chores to the child's schedule, and the days quickly get pretty full.

Too Much Too Soon   In his groundbreaking book *The Hurried Child*, Dr. David Elkind argued that parents are pushing children to grow up too fast. We expect too much of them, give them too much, and throw too many things at them before the children are mature enough to handle it all. The result is a generation, or generations, of children growing up under a great deal of stress which they do not understand and cannot cope with very well. These children are not allowed the opportunity to simply be children and develop naturally, at their own pace, as most children have in the past.

No Time to Be a Family

It is not only children who live busy and hurried lives, but their parents as well. This phenomenon has profound implications for the lives of families and children. Mary Zesiewicz, M.D., in her book *Fast Forwarding Through Childhood* discusses how many children experience a sense of being rejected and abandoned by parents who are on the "fast track" in life. While the parents are working hard to succeed in their careers, traveling, working late, and accomplishing impressive things, the children are missing the attention, nurturing, and simple presence of their parents to the extent that they may feel emotionally abandoned. These feelings of abandonment intensify the anxiety the children already feel from the many stressors that everyday life places on them.

Being placed in inadequately staffed day care centers at an early age, coming home to an empty house or a babysitter, and being rushed from one activity to another makes it impossible to spend enough time with parents who are themselves living a hurried lifestyle. There may be some time to talk in the car, during mealtimes (if the family eats meals together, no sure thing these days), or at bedtime. Being pushed to compete and achieve from an early age, at the expense of sharing fun and relaxing time with family and peers, can also add to a sense of emotional unfullfilment. Does playing in another basketball game really benefit the child as much as renting a movie, making some popcorn, and spending a relaxing evening at home with the family? Many children I know, and have worked with, would gladly opt for the movie, popcorn, and relaxed family time.

The Problems of the Stressed-Out Child

Kids need free time, unstructured playtime, to "decompress" and relax. It is during this free time that they are most likely to develop creative, independent thinking, to use the powers of their imaginations and let their thoughts roam. This is also key time in developing relationships with peers, when the kids are free to simply be themselves and not be instructed, coached, or closely supervised by an adult. Teenagers also need to "kick back" and take time for themselves. When this free time is not available, children's ability to manage stress decreases, which leads to other problems as well.

What we have also witnessed along with an increasingly hurried lifestyle is a rise in health problems. There has been a steady rise in the past few decades in the incidence of depression among children. In addition, depression has gotten more severe and strikes people at a younger age. Whereas depression used to affect predominantly middle-aged women in the first half of the twentieth century, now it strikes significant numbers of young adults, teens, and children. A recent large-scale study involving 3,000 children between the ages of twelve and fourteen found that, surprisingly, fully 9 percent of these children had depression severe enough to be diagnosed as a depressive disorder (Lewinsohn, et al., 1993). These are new and troubling changes in the lives of children, as the noted psychologist Martin Seligman points out in *The Optimistic Child*. Indeed the phenomenon is being described as an epidemic of depression among children, adolescents, and young adults. Some of the ramifications include increased rates of suicide, more alcohol and other drug use, and higher rates of school failure and dropouts.

The Kiddie Fast Track   Children caught up in a hurried lifestyle of nonstop activity have decreased opportunity to obtain the attention and nurturing they want, or to develop a close and trusting relationship with a parent where difficult issues and problems can be openly discussed. At the same time, more demands are placed on them. Mary Zesiewicz discusses some of these demands in *Fast Forwarding Through Childhood*. Children are starting school at a younger age, beginning with preschool. This can be a source of stress for many youngsters, who may simply not be emotionally mature enough for that type of experience. Many children are placed in substandard day care centers, which are understaffed and employ poorly trained, low-paid childcare workers. Schools are giving more homework, starting in younger grades. Many kindergarten classes teach academic material that used to be taught in first grade, and assign homework regularly. What's wrong, many parents are asking, with keeping kindergarten a time for play, for learning some of the arts in fun ways, and allowing the children to build social skills from interacting with peers? Who took the fun out of kindergarten, and why?

Chronic, excessive stress leads to a wide range of emotional and physical disorders. Depression may be one, as discussed earlier, and may become severe enough to wreak havoc in the person's life. An alarming feature of depression in childhood is that these children will be more likely to develop depression in adulthood also, setting the stage for a lifetime of unhappiness and problems. Phobias, panic disorder, and other anxiety disorders are associated with high levels of stress. Bulimia, anorexia, and other eating disorders are also more likely to develop. Alcohol and other drug abuse are sometimes used to escape or self-medicate, then take on a life of their own when the person develops an addiction. Physical problems such as heart disease, high blood pressure, migraine headaches, high cholesterol, and even cancer are all stress-related disorders.

Stress Reduction, Family Style

Families can be a source of stress, but also provide the best environment and most opportunities for dealing with stress and the many challenges in life. Children need a place to be safe, accepted, and secure. They need to feel loved for who they are, not for their grades, sports trophies, popularity among peers, or other achievements. The family needs to be a place where one is allowed to be herself or himself, without being judged, having to prove one's worth, or having to earn one's status as a family member. How many other social institutions besides the family can provide this opportunity? Children need a sense of belonging to a larger whole, a group that provides them with safety, nurturing, values, and a sense of identity that goes beyond their individual identities. The family still serves this function better than any other institution. When children or young adults don't get these needs met in their immediate family, or don't have a stable family to belong to, they are more likely to try and fulfill these needs within the artificial family atmosphere of a gang, a cult, or other subculture group. The need to belong, to be accepted, and to be with people who care about you is a universal need.

Have a Healthy Marriage   To start with, one thing parents can do to help provide for their children's security needs is to build a caring and stable marital relationship. It's been said that one of the best things parents can do for their children is to love one another. While this may sound quaint and somewhat old-fashioned, it is still as true as ever. A stable, loving marriage provides a bedrock of emotional stability for every member of the family. The opposite is also true, namely that a shaky, conflictual, or dishonest marriage can be extremely stressful for everyone in the family. The incidence of children's emotional, behavioral, academic, and even physical problems goes up when marital problems become bad or worsen. When parents are stressed and hurting they are more likely to withdraw, becoming less attuned and less attentive to the children. If the marriage falls apart and divorce is imminent, children are even more likely to fall apart as well and have increased emotional and behavioral problems. One frequent recommendation for a family going through a divorce is to seek helpful counseling or therapy, to help manage the stressors and emotional trauma that can almost be predicted in advance.

Allow Time for Doing Nothing   One of the most basic strategies to reduce stress is to allow for "downtime" when nothing is expected and people can do whatever they want. This most basic of human needs gets little respect in our hurried-up society, which is precisely part of the problem. During downtime nothing is expected in terms of work or responsibility, and performance or results are not demanded. Children can be asked if they want to do something recreational, or simply be told to "go and play." What about chores? There are few chores that cannot wait for a day now and then, or even half a day. If you want to be a creative parent, reward your kids sometimes by giving them a coupon for a "No Chores Day" and let them loaf around. Their smiles will tell you how much they value this temporary respite from responsibilities and demands on them. Won't this encourage the children to be lazy and irresponsible, some parents might wonder? Of course not. On the contrary, you would be teaching your children a centuries-old coping skill that used to be called "rest." As our ancestors knew long before we came along, rest is one of the best stress reducers. Even the Almighty in the Judeo-Christian tradition rested on the seventh day, and it seems very unlikely that such behavior was looked upon as lazy, irresponsible, or procrastinating.

Give Hugs   A terrific stress reducer for children (and adults!) is simple, spontaneous, affectionate touching and physical contact. Few things in life can warm a person on the inside like a loving and sincere hug. When children are hurt, sad, lonely, or feeling disappointed over something that happened in their lives, often the best things to provide them are a warm hug and a listening ear. Touch is as basic and important a need for human beings as food. When parents and children don't spend much time together, there are simply not enough opportunities for talking, touching, soothing, reassuring, and expressing interest and affection in hundreds of small ways. There is no substitute for this time spent together—it is a requirement for developing warm and loving relationships with children. The convenient myth of "quality time," where busy parents supposedly can spend less time with their children if they make their time together "quality" time, has turned out to be exactly that, a myth. My guess is that most children saw through this myth long before their parents did.

Build Self-esteem   Children who have a strong sense of self-esteem and feel competent to deal with the challenges in their lives, are much more capable of dealing with stress. These children are not immune to stress, but simply more resistant to it and much better at avoiding the problems associated with stress. There are constructive things that parents can do to help foster self-esteem in their children—this is discussed in more detail in chapter 11 of this book, entitled *How to Nurture Self-esteem: The P.A.S. Model.* In part, self-esteem evolves naturally from secure and loving relationships. Parents, teachers, and other caretakers can also play active roles in building self-esteem by helping children develop skills and a genuine sense of competence that comes from accomplishing real tasks.

The Search for Balance

Managing stress effectively in the long run, for parents as well as children, requires building a healthy lifestyle and then maintaining that as a way of everyday life. A healthy diet and regular exercise program can help a great deal in controlling stress. So can meditation, yoga, and spiritual contemplation. Too much alcohol or caffeine consumption leaves us feeling more stressed, not less. Having too many things on our agenda requires that we cut back on our commitments and leave more time for ourselves and our family. Having work responsibilities intrude into our home and family life requires that we manage our jobs better, and learn how to put our job aside when we walk into our home. If that is not possible and this remains a persistent problem, perhaps finding a new job might be the solution. The alternative could be sacrificing your peace of mind, your health, and quite possibly your family's well-being—what income level or prestige position is worth making those sacrifices?

Chapter **9**

"Do As I Say, Not As I Do"

"Children are natural mimics—they act like their parents
in spite of every attempt to teach them good manners."

—*Anonymous*

This chapter is about parenting, but mostly it's about what kind of parent you want to be. If we make the question a little broader, what kind of person do you want to be? Those two questions will go a long way in determining what influence you have on your children, and what kinds of lessons they learn from you. Children are natural mimics, as the humorous quotation above indicates, and very good ones at that. What they learn from watching us are not only behaviors and mannerisms, but at a much deeper level they pick up values, perceptions, prejudices, expectations, and certain ways of looking at the world and dealing with life. The old truism that "the apple does not fall far from the tree" has its basis not only in biology and genetics, but also just as much in learned behaviors. Children are more influenced by their parents' behavior than by anyone else.

DON'T BE A POOR ROLE MODEL

The popular media defines "role model" as a person who is looked up to, admired, and imitated for their celebrity or hero-worship status. This celebrity concept of a role model is usually reserved for sports stars, movie stars, music stars, and so on. The psychological definition of role model is broader than this, and defines a role model simply as any person who serves as a model for another person to learn from, imitate, and strive to be like. Hero worship is not implied nor necessary. This definition is much more useful in helping us to understand how children learn.

The Power of Imitation and Identification

Children begin to imitate others during the second year of life. As social learning theories of childhood development tell us, not all behaviors that children observe will be imitated, of course. Behavior is more likely to be imitated if it occurs consistently, and the person being observed is someone whom the child feels attached to. Second, the behavior may not be imitated right away, but processed internally in the child's mind and put away for later use. This is an important point to keep in mind because the capacity for delayed imitation means the child can pick up aggressive, abusive, or manipulative behavior from watching the parent and not demonstrate it until months or years down the road. Third, the observed consequences of the behavior will also help determine if it is imitated by the child. If the child sees the behavior getting approval, or results, it will be more likely to be repeated. Finally, the behaviors are more likely to be imitated if they fit within a consistent set of values or expectations, and if the model is a person who is perceived as powerful or high in status. Most or all of these features are commonly found in parent-child relationships, which make the parent a powerful role model for the child.

In addition to imitation, there is another process that goes on in children's social and emotional development that psychologists call identification. This process, originally noted by Sigmund Freud, describes how a child incorporates characteristics of another person by adopting that person's attitudes, interests, values, and patterns of thought and behavior. As with imitation, the child is more likely to identify with a person where there are feelings of warmth and closeness, and the person is perceived as being important and powerful. Again, parents fit the bill, and the child is more likely to identify with a parent than with other people, particularly in young childhood.

Parents Are the Natural Role Models

All parents, as long as they are part of their children's lives, are role models for their children. This is not a matter of choice, but rather it happens because human nature makes us that way. Parents will influence children in both positive and negative ways; the only sure thing is that the influence will be there. How parents exert their influence will depend partly on what they express and communicate verbally to their children. Much of the communication that goes on between human beings, however, particularly in the complex emotional context of a family, is communicated on a nonverbal level. Both imitation and identification happen naturally, without either the child or the parent needing to plan it or even be aware of it.

Children pick up values and complex ways of looking at the world from their relationships with parents and other primary caretakers. The teaching of values cannot be taught directly, simply by telling a child which values he or she should believe in. As Dr. Haim Ginott writes in *Between Parent and Child*, values "are absorbed, and become part of the child, only through his identification with, and emulation of, persons who gain his love and respect." A child's value system is built and evolves over time based on living within a family and community that holds a set of values and lives them out through behavior. A child is more likely to identify with, imitate, and emulate a parent more strongly than any other person. Behavior speaks more powerfully than words. If you as a parent wish your children to hold certain values and behave in certain ways, the most powerful message to the child is to model those behaviors yourself and live them in your everyday life.

The Changing Faces of Parental Role Models

The exact manner in which children relate to their parents as role models depends to some degree on the child's maturational level. Most young children look up to their parents in a kind of idealized, hero-worship manner, convinced that the parents know everything and are capable of doing anything. This perception of the all-knowing and all-powerful parent does not survive for long. By their preadolescent years, children realize that parents are only human, and have flaws, weaknesses, and problems along with their positive qualities. This may be disillusioning to an extent, but certainly does not have to cause problems. Parents for the most part are still viewed as loving, well-intentioned people who deserve respect and cooperation. The need to have an idealized role model to look up to switches focus to music stars, sports stars, and other celebrities, or to a teacher, coach, or relative. This is normal and should not be a cause for alarm. Eventually, the kids learn that media stars and other personal heroes are flawed and imperfect human beings, like everyone else.

The Picture of Parents By their teen years, when adolescents are struggling with issues of developing their own identities and more independence from parents, the parents may become figures who are tolerated more than admired. Amazingly, the same parent who seven or ten years ago was a benevolent and wise parent becomes transformed into a poorly informed, unhip individual who is hopelessly behind the times. Even worse, the parent may be perceived as a controlling dictator who is a threat to the teenager's need for independence and freedom. Is it any wonder that parents and teens have more conflicts, disagreements, and arguments during this stage of development?

By early adulthood, children regain a more positive outlook on their parents, and greater appreciation of the qualities that made their parents such admirable and terrific people in the first place. Mark Twain made this point beautifully in his well-known quotation about learning to appreciate his father: "When I was a boy of fourteen, my father was so ignorant I could hardly stand to have the old man around. But when I got to be twenty-one, I was astonished at how much the old man had learned in seven years" (Mark Twain, in *Notes*, reprinted in *601 Quotes About Marriage & Family*). This understanding and appreciation of one's parents comes with maturity and the resolution of the child's needs for separation and independence. It is not something that can be rushed, nor should it be argued about.

Being a Positive Role Model

Good parents are natural positive role models. The values they hold dear come out spontaneously in their behavior, day in and day out. Does that mean parents need to be perfect examples of virtuous living, always saying and doing the right things? Of course not. Being human means being imperfect, making mistakes, and falling far short of the standards of perfection. There are certain basic qualities that make a parent, or for that matter any person, a good role model for children. Some of these are briefly discussed below.

Be Human It is never a good idea to expect perfection in oneself, and certainly not in one's children. Perfectionists wind up as tense, anxious people who see themselves as failing in life. Accept the reality of being an imperfect human being, and accept it in others as well. Be willing to admit when you are wrong. Offer a sincere apology if appropriate. Take responsibility for your mistakes, and make amends for any harm done if that is called for. Forgive mistakes in others, particularly children, if the mistakes are not malicious and the person assumes responsibility.

Be Honest Children recognize and respect honesty and integrity, and most children have an uncanny ability to smell out hypocrisy. Hypocrisy kills trust as well as respect. Don't sneak and hide doing irresponsible things, if you want your children to be honest with you about their behavior. Be open and direct about feelings, if you want them to share feelings with you. Express wishes directly so they know what you expect of them, and so they share their wishes and needs with you. Don't talk about other people behind their backs, particularly family members.

Be Responsible   Take care of things you need to do, in your job and your family. Keep your promises. Never make a promise you don't intend to keep. Don't take on more responsibilities than you can handle. Be where you are supposed to be, on time. Follow through. Make yourself available to your family, particularly to young children who need and crave their parents' attention.

Be Considerate   Become a good listener and hear the other person out, even if the other person is five years old. Treat others with respect, if you demand respectful behavior from your children. Don't belittle or criticize others, and certainly not your child. A child who is repeatedly criticized for his behavior does not learn responsible behavior, but rather learns to criticize others and to condemn himself for his faults. Don't call names, even in joking, because negative labels have a way of cutting deep and being remembered for a long time. Don't shame others. Don't be a bully, unless you want your child to become a bully also.

Being a Poor Role Model

What makes a parent a poor role model? In general, expecting your children to do things different from you is unrealistic and, let's face it, an exercise in hypocrisy. The injunction to "do as I say, not as I do" has never worked, and never will. Engaging in self-destructive behaviors such as drinking excessively or using other drugs provides very bad examples for your children, obviously. It does not help to tell your children that such behavior is wrong and therefore they should not do it—you, mom and dad, have to walk the walk, not just talk the talk. Poor role modeling occurs when a parent has trouble managing his or her anger, but expects the children not to lose control of their anger. When parents keep secrets from one another, even in seemingly innocuous ways such as telling a child "don't tell daddy that I bought this" or "don't tell mommy that I broke the vase," it becomes difficult to expect the child to appreciate the values of honesty. The bottom line is, if you don't want your children to engage in certain negative behaviors, don't engage in them yourself.

Parental Hypocrisy Doesn't Work It sends a mixed message to children that is confusing and creates internal, emotional conflicts for them. When a parents' verbal message does not match up with the parents' behavior, the behavioral message will make the bigger impact. Most children are idealistic. They want to be "good," and expect their parents to act in responsible and mature ways also and do the "right" thing. When parents behave in a hypocritical manner, children will most likely respond in one of two ways. The more independent child might resent the parents' behavior and rebel against it. The alternative is to identify with the parent and imitate the parents' negative behavior. For most children, the common response is to imitate, because it is less threatening emotionally than it would be to challenge the parent. When this happens, both the parent and the child lose.

The musician Cat Stevens wrote a song called *Cat in the Cradle* which first became popular in the 1970s, and still gets playing time on some music stations. This plaintive song tells the story of a boy who keeps asking his dad to spend time with him and do things together. The father is of course very busy, and keeps making promises of spending time with the boy in the future: "I'm sorry, son, I really don't know when, but we'll get together then, yeah, you know we'll have a good time then." Eventually the son grows up and moves away. Now it becomes the father's turn to ask his son when they can spend some time together. The busy son ends up making promises to the father: "I'm sorry, dad, I really don't know when, but we'll get together then, yeah, you know we'll have a good time then." At the song's sad conclusion the father realizes just how much the son learned from his behavior: "He'd grown up just like me, yeah, my boy was just like me." This song put a lump in the throats of many dads, and well it should. It would be good to make it required listening for all parents, fathers and mothers alike.

Chapter **10**

"Don't Worry, He'll Grow Out of It"

All good parents want the best for their children. When they're born, we are full of excitement and high hopes for them. We are relieved and grateful they're born healthy. We fuss and worry over them when they get sick, fall and skin their knees, or cut a finger on a sharp object. We want our children to be okay, well adjusted, successful, and happy. We want them to have a healthy childhood, do well in school, have friends, stay away from drugs, and get through adolescence without the major problems which teens are prone to. We want them to have a successful college career, a job that provides a good income, and happiness in a loving and stable relationship.

IS THAT TOO MUCH TO ASK?

Sometimes the answer is "yes." Kids being kids, in other words just normal human beings, they will encounter their share (or more) of problems and difficulties in life. Common sense and statistics from doctors, schools, and police departments tell us that. As parents, however, our hope is that those bad things never happen to *our* kids. Other kids get in trouble with the law, not our Jimmy. Other kids drink and use drugs, not our Sara. It's not that we wish bad things on those "other" kids of course, just that the thought of our children having serious problems scares us and makes us worry.

Don't Deny Serious Problems

Positive thinking and wishing for the best is a wonderful thing that helps us meet the challenges of life; however, this is true only up to a point. Denial is the extreme, unhealthy result of trying too hard to look on the bright side—it involves losing our healthy ability to see and recognize a real problem. Denial is not only unhealthy, it can be very destructive and even dangerous. The stories of Erica and Jason (see p. 210) tell of two different types of problems involving denial, and sadly of two different outcomes.

Erica's Story

Mr. and Mrs. Brown came to my office because they and their eleven-year-old daughter Erica were having constant battles over homework and lack of responsibility. I spoke with the parents first to get the background information. Both parents were successful professionals in their early forties. Erica was the younger of two children. Her thirteen-year-old brother Dan was an honor roll student, popular at school, and generally well behaved at home. Erica on the other hand struggled with schoolwork since the fourth grade, and drove her parents nuts at home. She was missing assignments, turning in sloppy or incomplete work, was very disorganized, and performing far below her ability level. Her inconsistent effort and sloppy work hurt her grades of course, which was the topic of many lectures and talks. There seemed to be little pattern to her up and down performance in school, which was frustrating for Erica, her parents, and her teachers.

Report card time had become an occasion Erica and her parents learned to dread. Predictably it was an occasion for disappointment, lectures, threats, promises, and often angry arguments. This was very stressful for all of them. Erica wanted to do well, make her parents happy, and keep up with her friends who were all good students. They discussed what she needed to do in order to improve, and Erica made sincere promises to change her behavior. The following semester, however, the same pattern would be repeated. She started out well in the beginning, then became more disorganized, started missing work, and seemed to stop trying as hard. She sometimes lied to her parents to cover up her failures. The lying only made things worse, which they told her many times, at first with sympathy and then with anger and laying down severe consequences. Lying would not be tolerated, her behavior would improve, and that was that.

"Her lack of motivation and lying to us is so frustrating," Erica's mother said, her voice rising in exasperation. "We don't know what to do with her anymore." Her father saw her primarily as being immature and spoiled. "We give these kids so much these days," he lamented. "She doesn't see a reason to work for anything." When it was pointed out that their son also benefited from his parents' generosity, the dad shrugged his shoulders. Dan is much more mature, as his behavior showed. Erica just had a lot of growing up to do. She would grow out of this. Furthermore, the father was not even sure why they were sitting in a psychologist's office.

Listen to the Child

Erica was called in next while her parents waited for her in the waiting room. She was friendly and personable, bright, with lively and inquisitive blue eyes. Erica communicated easily and freely about a variety of topics. She was honest about her problems at school, and in fact seemed embarrassed by them. She knew that she could do better "if I tried harder." This message had been drummed into her hundreds, perhaps thousands of times. She cannot say what stops her from putting in effort consistently. "I'm just lazy," she said and her voice turned a sadder tone. What does it mean to be "lazy," I asked her. "It means that I'm not doing my work." Her label for herself of being "lazy" really tells us nothing, and certainly does not explain her difficulties. I have a rule in my office, I told her. People have to throw out of their vocabulary the word "lazy." Her bright smile indicated that she would be quite relieved and delighted to do just that!

As Erica talked about her experiences at school, home, and with her peers, it became clear that she cared a great deal and in fact set pretty high goals for herself. Lack of motivation was not the problem here. She was cooperative in class but very easily bored. Her mind wandered, she would daydream often, and got easily distracted by those around her. She was fidgety sometimes but not really hyper, like some kids who can't sit still. She talked too much in class, until the teacher reminded her once again to stop. She was not trying to be disruptive, she just "forgot" that she was not supposed to talk in class! Her two best friends called her "Chatty Kathy." It was difficult for her to sit in one place for a long time, or to do one thing for long. Lunchtime was a big relief, as was the bell at the end of the school day. She rushed to leave school and did not check her assignment list or books carefully to see that she had everything she needed.

When Effort Is Not Enough

At home she needed reminders to do her homework. She knew that homework was important, but there were always a thousand other things to think about and her mind jumped around a lot from one thing to another. When she finally hit the books she could read or study for about fifteen minutes before her mind "starts to drift." It was hard for her to stick with one thing until it got done. Some assignments didn't get completed because she did them part way, got distracted or interrupted, and was off to something else. Once she was done with an assignment it was quickly forgotten, as if it never existed. Many times she would complete the work but forget to turn it in. The assignment ended up in a pile of papers, or a book or folder somewhere, and Erica would get a zero for the missing assignment. She did not plan ahead for doing large projects and always had to rush at the last minute. She had regular household chores such as feeding the dog and picking up in her room, but often forgot to do these chores and had to be reminded by her parents. When they got tired of reminding her, tempers flared. They were tired of her being irresponsible. She was tired of them picking on her.

In the next conversation with the Browns, it was suggested that Erica's problem behaviors were not due to immaturity, defiance, or lack of motivation. Rather, her behavior, which started when she was very young, fit the profile of a person with Attention Deficit Disorder, or ADD for short. We would need to do some testing to be certain. If it turned out that she did indeed have ADD, this was a very treatable condition that can be managed affectively through behavioral techniques and sometimes medication.

"Not My Child"

Mrs. Brown looked disbelieving. One of her nephews was diagnosed with ADD and was being treated with medication. He was hyper and disruptive, and Erica was nothing like that. Erica's father looked upset. He wanted his daughter to improve her behavior, not to find new excuses for it. She made enough excuses as it was! He also remembered a television news segment on ADD not long ago. One of the people being interviewed made the statement that "every time a kid jumps up and down three times he's diagnosed with ADD and put on Ritalin." This was ridiculous! His daughter did not have ADD, and she was not going to be placed on drugs. They promised to consider my recommendations if the problems did not improve.

This is not an uncommon reaction of many parents when faced with the possibility that their child is having a problem that goes beyond the usual realm of difficulties kids experience in growing up. Some parents end up simply dismissing the doctor's opinion. They go back to what they had been doing, convinced they wasted their time and money on getting a "quack" opinion. They know things would be fine if the child tried harder, listened to them more, spent less time watching TV, ate less sugar, did not hang around with the friend who was a bad influence, or simply "grew up."

I heard from Mr. and Mrs. Brown again five months later. Erica's behavior had gotten worse, and their arguments more frequent and angry. She was beginning to openly defy her mother when asked to do things around the house. The lying about schoolwork continued. She was obviously feeling stressed about her academic problems, and was lying to cover up problems or to postpone dealing with the consequences. Events reached a boiling point after Erica was grounded from the TV for three weeks, and then from the phone for two weeks. When confronted about missing schoolwork again she went into a rage, screamed at her mother, and threw her math book against the wall so hard it knocked off a picture three feet away.

Confronting the Problem   Psychological testing showed that Erica was in the top 1 percent of kids her age in having problems with distractibility, staying focused, listening, difficulty organizing tasks, losing things, forgetting, and avoiding tasks that required sustained concentration and effort. In other words, she had Attention Deficit Disorder without the physically hyperactive component. She was simply not able to do the things asked of her, no matter how hard she tried or how badly she wanted to succeed. The problem was not a lack of motivation, bad parents, or bad teachers, but a biological problem called ADD that affects brain functioning in the areas of attention, impulsivity, and sometimes physical restlessness and hyperactive behavior.

Erica's behavior improved markedly after her physician found a medication that worked well for her ADD symptoms, and she learned behavioral coping skills in therapy. Once the pressure was off, the tension level at home dropped dramatically as well. Erica was fortunate because her parents sought help and their denial only lasted a few months. Many people with ADD go into their late teens, twenties, thirties, forties, and late adulthood without the condition being diagnosed and treated. Sometimes the problem is a lack of information. Sometimes denial is the problem, on the part of the parents or on the part of the adult with ADD.

The Path of Denial

It is very uncomfortable emotionally for many parents to view their child as not being "normal," or as being flawed in some way. When a child has a serious problem it can bring up a sense of guilt or shame in the parent. Did I cause this problem by being a bad parent? Am I to blame for passing on "bad" genes to my child? And what will the relatives think? It is common for parents to wish, even if it's a secret wish kept deep inside, for their children to be perfect. Or, if he or she is not perfect, then at least not to have any serious problems. This wish can profoundly affect our perceptions and even our judgment. That is the core of denial.

The Price of Denial

At its worst, denial prevents a problem from being treated and resolved. Often this means the problem will likely get worse over time. The price paid by the child is one of continued struggling or suffering when the problem is related to a condition that the child will not "grow out of." Such pervasive conditions include learning disabilities such as dyslexia, attention deficit disorder, emotional problems such as childhood depression or anxiety disorder, or problems with drinking and other types of substance abuse. Sometimes the problems being denied are serious medical conditions which can become life threatening. Denial usually hurts. Sometimes it can kill.

The wise parent will accept a child as a normal human being with strengths and weaknesses, good points and bad, triumphs and failures, periods of dealing with problems and getting into things that are not good for them. Having one or more of these problems does not make the child any less "normal"—quite the contrary, the normal thing is to experience problems in life. The healthy thing is to deal with those problems as openly, honestly, and effectively as possible. As parents we need to manage our fears and anxieties about our children by dealing with problems directly, not wishing that they did not exist.

Chapter **11**

How to Nurture Self-esteem: The P.A.S. Model

S elf-esteem is a concept that is both widely used and often misunderstood in popular culture. Robbie's parents are told that he is doing poorly in school because he has poor self-esteem and does not apply himself, for example. Monica is shy with children her age and has difficulty making friends due to fear of rejection and low self-esteem. George's mom is reluctant to start her own business because she doubts her ability to manage it well and make it successful. Does she lack self-esteem? There are numerous self-help books and motivational tapes on the topic of self-esteem, providing advice and inspirational messages about how to think positively and feel happy with oneself. Just build up your self-esteem and you can conquer the world, the underlying messages seem to say.

DON'T NEGLECT YOUR CHILD'S EMOTIONAL GROWTH

As most people discover, the benefits of inspirational messages and pep talks don't last very long and provide temporary relief at best. This is true whether the messages come from a book, a tape, or a concerned friend or family member. The simple reason for this is that building self-esteem involves much more than talking or thinking about it. Helping children develop self-esteem requires more than telling a child that she or he is a wonderful and special person, although compliments are certainly a good start if communicated sincerely and with affection.

Achievement Is Not Enough

In this chapter I will propose a three-part model for helping children (and adults) feel good about themselves and build a strong sense of self-esteem that lasts a lifetime. The first factor involves a core set of positive *perceptions* and beliefs about oneself, based on a realistic appraisal of a person's actual abilities and positive qualities. The second factor involves attaining a satisfying level of *achievement,* mastering skills and finding areas of competence where the person gains genuine successes. The third factor involves a strong family-based emotional *support* system where the person is accepted, nurtured, and indeed esteemed. This third factor is often underestimated or simply overlooked, but in my opinion it is a crucial one given the social and emotional nature of human beings.

All three components of self-esteem that make up this model—Perception, Achievement, and Support—are essential in providing a person with a sense of being good, competent, successful, valued, and loved. The combined affects of these three factors or components provide a solid foundation for genuine and lasting self-esteem. If any of these components are missing, a person will likely struggle with issues of self-worth and self-satisfaction. The family in general and parents in particular can play a vital role in developing all three of these areas of self-esteem. How that can be done is the focus of this chapter.

What Is Self-Esteem?

By the age of two, children develop concepts about who they are and what they are like. The child develops a general sense of self that includes awareness of being male or female, belonging within a family, liking or disliking certain foods, having favorite toys or games, and so on. This general self-concept is descriptive rather than judgmental. Self-esteem, which refers to a person's evaluation of her or his abilities or personal qualities, does not develop until later years. When a young child performs a self-evaluation, those are limited to a specific task or situation. For example, a child can view herself as being good at sports, terrible at spelling, okay at playing video games, and great at making friends. Ask a child younger than seven if he "feels good" about himself, and you will likely get a confused look. Before the age of seven or eight, children have expectations about being good or bad at some specific task, but no generalized sense of self-esteem.

Global Goodness   By the age of eight or nine, a child develops a more general sense of competence and self-worth. In the process of forming perceptions, concepts, and a sense of identity about themselves, children attribute good or bad qualities to themselves. The sum of all these self-evaluations make up the child's sense of self-esteem. It should be kept in mind that self-esteem remains domain specific to some extent. Confidence in sports does not necessarily translate to a sense of competence and optimism in math class, for example. Similarly, the student who shines in math may not feel confident nor secure on the baseball field, or in a group social situation. There is however a global sense we all have of how "good" a person we are, which comes from the attitudes and feelings we have about ourselves, and which can profoundly influence our behavior.

While self-esteem as a concept may be tricky to define, almost everyone has an intuitive grasp of what it involves. When we get to know a person with high self-esteem, we know it. Similarly, when we get to know a person with low self-esteem, we can sense that also in different ways. Sometimes strong impressions are made even during the initial meeting. The individual's body language, manner of communicating, ease and comfort with themselves, eye contact, and level of assertiveness all may communicate something about the person's level of self-esteem.

The Role of Positive Perceptions in Self-esteem

Self-esteem starts with positive perceptions and beliefs about oneself. We begin to form those perceptions at a young age from the comments and feedback we get from others. Parents are usually the first and most intimate communicators of verbal messages to children. Because there is a natural emotional bond between parent and child, a parent's comments are more likely to be taken to heart by the child than comments from other people. What an opportunity this is for the parent to point out and express appreciation for the child's positive qualities and good behaviors. These expressions are most effective when they are spontaneous, sincere, and communicated with affection. Exaggeration and insincerity are not necessary, and in fact will do more harm than good.

Does the child stand up for what she believes? Express appreciation for that, and acknowledge the courage it takes to assert oneself when others disagree. Does he tell really good jokes and make you laugh? Let him know that, and tell a few jokes in return. Does she use good manners when you visit a relative's house? Praise her good manners and consideration for others. Did he do a good job cleaning up the toys after his friend left? Let him know that, and give him an extra fifteen minutes of TV time tonight. Did she study hard for the spelling test? Let her know that you see and appreciate her good effort, and are proud of her attitude toward schoolwork. Is he good at shooting a basketball? Take some extra time to shoot baskets on the weekend, and see if he wants to join the little league basketball team. Does she have a great ear for music? Show your admiration for it, praise her to the relatives and neighbors, and discuss whether she is interested in taking music lessons. All of these parental acknowledgments of a child's good qualities, good effort, and interest in developing talents and skills create an impact on the child's perceptions of himself. The child incorporates positive, healthy perceptions of herself into her image of who she is. These positive perceptions serve as building blocks in developing self-esteem.

Praising Real Effort Little comments made throughout the day add up over weeks, months, and years to convey a consistent and powerful message. The child whose parents acknowledge and praise his effort on a school project will take pride in his effort, and will thus be more likely to work hard on the next assignment as well. Doing well on the assignment will motivate good effort in the future, earning the child further praise from the parents. Most important, this process shapes the child's perception of himself as a responsible student who tries hard on school assignments and makes his parents proud. This positive image the child builds in his mind affects his attitude toward school, responsibility, parents, and self. The achievement that comes from his good effort builds a sense of competence that is more meaningful than ten statements of "you are smart" which are not connected to an actual achievement. The affection, gladness, and pride shown toward the child by her parent builds a sense of being accepted, liked, admired, and loved.

Contrast the scenario above with the case of another child whose parent takes his effort for granted, ignores it because the parent is unavailable and uninvolved, or even worse belittles it as not a big deal or not being good enough. Which child is more likely to have confidence in her abilities, expectations of being competent and successful, and a positive attitude toward school? All of these things will ultimately impact the child's self-esteem, in either a positive or negative manner. The parent can steer the direction of the child's perceptions, opinions, and expectations, as well as the child's present and future behavior. The child who perceives himself as being a hard worker and competent student, whose efforts will be rewarded, will likely try to live up to that image in the future. The child who is not as certain about her level of competence, or expects that her efforts may not be noticed or appreciated, will likely live up to these expectations also with the result being inconsistent effort and spotty achievement.

Lovable Qualities The general goal in helping a child build self-esteem through positive perceptions is to acknowledge the child's good qualities, strengths, and worth. This does not mean that problem behaviors should be overlooked or not dealt with. Stealing, lying, destructive behavior, underage drinking, and other bad behavior should be disciplined fairly and consistently, but always with the expectation that the child is capable of better and indeed that the parent expects the child to behave better in the future. It is very possible to acknowledge and deal with problems while still affirming that the children's faults and problems are outweighed by their positive qualities, responsible behaviors, and lovable nature. The general emphasis still can be on strengths more than on faults, and praising good behaviors more than scolding bad behaviors.

The Role of Achievement in Self-esteem

The self-esteem movement in this country placed a strong focus on the cognitive, belief-based component of self-esteem discussed above. Parents and teachers were encouraged to help children build self-esteem by telling them they are good, smart, talented, creative, special, unique, and so on. This approach is not successful in and of itself in raising self-esteem, and in some ways can cause problems when overdone or carried to an extreme. Having a child write the words "I am special" twenty times on a sheet of paper will not persuade the child that he is special. It will certainly not create self-esteem in any meaningful way. Positive affirmations are most effective when they are sincere, come from a person whom the child values and respects, and are tied to real achievements, talents, or qualities.

While it is sometimes true that children will believe what they are told if they hear it often enough, this usually applies to things that are not too obvious or cannot be easily proved or disproved. Sadly it applies well to cases of abuse, where the child cannot easily disprove abusive messages such as "you are bad," "you are stupid," or "you will never amount to anything." Repeatedly making positive assertions to children that may not be true can cause problems as well if those assertions turn out to be false. Children may be idealistic and impressionable, but they cannot be fooled forever by undeserving or insincere praise. If the children don't experience their share of success, at school, socially, and within the family, the accolades will ring hollow and cheapen the value of compliments which *are* deserved, and possibly set up the child for a shock later when she realizes her true talents and accomplishments.

In short, positive messages and words are not enough. Children need to build confidence and self-esteem based on actual achievements as well. Psychologist Martin Seligman made this point very succinctly in his book *The Optimistic Child*. Seligman argues that there are two aspects to self-esteem, a "feeling good" component and a "doing well" component. Without the "doing well" component, which involves building skills, mastering real problems, and achieving meaningful goals, the "feeling good" component cannot stand on its own. Eventually the verbal praise seems insincere, overdone, and manipulative, and even the kids see through it. If *everyone* is "special," Seligman points out as others have also done, then *nobody* is special because the term has lost its meaning.

Self-esteem Is a By-product of Success   In Seligman's view, self-esteem is thus a by-product of success, not the cause of it. Self-esteem is built on experiencing success and proving oneself competent, not from being told that one is competent and capable of success. It stands to reason then that feeling good about oneself cannot be achieved until a person is taught how to be successful and actually attains some real success. Seligman has little patience with the self-esteem movement advocates who tried to prevent school failure, drug abuse, teenage pregnancies, chronic dependence on welfare, and other social problems, by teaching self-esteem directly to children in school. To Seligman, this confuses the cause and effect. He writes: "Low self-esteem is a consequence of failing in school, of being on welfare, of being arrested—not the cause." The solutions then are to teach people how to succeed in school, get off welfare, and avoid behavior for which one can be arrested.

In *The Optimistic Child,* Dr. Seligman further argues that not only has the self-esteem movement failed to improve school performance by improving self-esteem, it has in fact backfired and caused children to become more disillusioned and depressed. Severe depression is much more common among children since the 1970s, and strikes children at younger ages. Whether or how much of that effect is due to the self-esteem movement is open for debate. There is little doubt however that an emphasis on feeling good, at the expense of doing well, is not the solution to fostering high self-esteem in children or in anyone else for that matter. Feeling good and doing well go together and feed off each other. Both are important.

In addition to the behavioral perspective that good feelings are the result of successes, and thus depend on doing well, Dr. Seligman also includes a cognitive component that influences self-esteem. When something bad happens, people try to determine the causes based on their particular explanatory style. A person who is pessimistic will blame themselves, believe that the problem will last forever, and believe that it will have profound negative effects on their life. A person who is an optimist will tend to blame some external factor in the world rather than blame themselves, will view the problem as temporary until a solution is found, and will view the damage as being limited rather than letting it ruin his life. Seligman believes that people can be taught to think more optimistically, which in turn will lead to greater effort, greater success, less giving up, and less depression. This cognitive approach has practical appeal and is used by many therapists. To the extent that it helps people to succeed, and helps them perceive themselves in a more positive light, it will help with self-esteem as well.

The Tools of Optimism and Realism The task for parents in helping their children in the "doing well" or achievement area is to help them maintain a sense of optimism and hope, maintain a high level of effort, and learn skills to overcome problems and accomplish tasks they need to accomplish. Part of doing well involves setting realistic, reasonable goals based on the person's actual abilities and talents. Being helpful in this case means setting limits at times and not allowing the child to overburden themselves to the point where failure is almost guaranteed. As optimistic and confident as the child might feel, playing two sports and also participating in the school play is too much for any twelve-year-old.

At times the child will need help with developing specific mastery skills, such as learning how to work with fractions, hit a baseball, or write a term paper. When a great deal of help is necessary and the parent lacks the skills, time, or patience required for the teaching, then hiring a tutor or instructor might be the best solution. Children need help with the things that don't come naturally to children, such as planning ahead, anticipating what needs to be done, and setting a schedule or timetable to accomplish a project. Most children need help with learning how to manage frustration, and persevering when they hit tough times. All of these skills will improve mastery and performance. Achieving real successes, as Dr. Seligman persuasively argues, also does wonders for improving self-esteem.

The Role of Family and Emotional Support in Self-esteem

There is a third component to self-esteem that is just as important as the cognitive and achievement factors, although it has been essentially overlooked by the self-esteem movement and the achievement based models. This has to do with having a healthy emotional support system in place, which in turn correlates strongly with high levels of acceptance and support within the family. Finding healthy amounts of support, affection, and acceptance within the family is not a luxury in developing self-esteem, but a vital necessity. Children know when they are loved, and feel worthwhile precisely because their parents love them and make them a priority in their lives. Growing up feeling loved creates positive feelings about oneself that goes very deep and lasts a lifetime. No amount of achievement, fame, or income level can compensate for this most basic of human emotional needs. If you ask people who are truly happy with themselves to define the sources of their happiness, family life and close personal relationships will be at or near the top of the list.

Teaching children how to think in positive ways and succeed at tasks or goals is still not sufficient to develop a strong sense of self-esteem. Children need to be loved, and to feel loved. They need emotional support to deal with the many disappointments and little failures that are almost a daily occurrence in life. This support and acceptance is not based on what a child does—we do not judge our children by their achievements, looks, talents, grades, popularity, or obedience to our wishes—but rather it is given to the child based simply on being part of the family. When a parent shows up at a ten-year-old's concert at school, the presence of the parent sends a message to the child that she is valued. The opposite effect is often painfully evident—the disappointment of the child when the parent does *not* show up. The loving parent will value that child's concert performance as much as the performance of a musician in the symphony orchestra, and perhaps more. The parents' approval and appreciation will certainly mean infinitely more to the hopeful, anxious, impressionable child, than to the professional musician who performs hundreds of such concerts.

Family Acceptance   Public adulation and support are based on what a person *does,* such as being a famous actor, musician, or sports star. Family acceptance and support are based simply on who the person *is,* namely a valued part of that family. One does not have to prove oneself to one's family, nor earn the love and support of family members. We do not love a child any greater because he is a good baseball player, and certainly don't love the child any less because his team finished last in little league baseball. This is as unconditional as love gets, and it does not have a counterpart in the social structure outside the family.

How can parents help create a supportive and loving family environment? This is a vital question that is answered in many ways, in different chapters and parts of this book. It starts with creating a sense of family identity, and then sticking together through thick and thin. It means making the family members the main focus of the family, not some career goal, financial goal, political goal, and so on. It means becoming committed to the well-being of each family member, and making the needs of each family member a priority. It involves family members treating each other with affection, speaking to each other with affection even when discipline or limits have to be enforced, and behaving affectionately in many simple ways on a day-to-day basis. It means affirming the worth of each person within the family, through words and actions, even when they disappoint or hurt us in the short term.

Continuing Acceptance Children need support even when they disagree with you, mom or dad, or when they do dumb things like coming home with a tattoo, or getting arrested for shoplifting. Being supportive of your child under trying conditions does not mean at all that you condone the shoplifting, criminal behavior, or poor judgment. It does mean that family loyalty and support means your child can count on you for guidance, advice, discipline, faith in his ability to learn from the mistake and behave better in the future, and most important your continuing love and acceptance. Be critical of the behavior and discipline as necessary, but love the child and demonstrate your faith in the child. That faith will contribute to the child's faith in himself to act responsibly, learn from mistakes, and overcome problems. It will help shape the child's perceptions of herself as someone who is basically a good person, with the ability to learn and grow, who is loved and valued by others. That child will be a person with a strong sense of self-esteem.

Creating a Family Atmosphere that Affirms and Supports

Dolores Curran, author of *Traits of a Healthy Family,* surveyed several hundred family professionals to try and determine what healthy families had in common. Not surprisingly her findings showed that families where members like each other, support each other, and bond together were the most happy and healthy. In interviewing many of these families she discovered that the children who seemed the happiest came from families that were the most affirming and supportive. Ms. Curran further outlined five traits or hallmarks of families that are most supportive, which are well worth reviewing here. Readers who wish a more detailed discussion are encouraged to read this very warm and practical book.

All Needs Considered First, the parents themselves have good self-esteem. They are not insecure or doubting about themselves. Parents who are excessively insecure will invariably communicate the insecurity to the children in some fashion. It becomes the parents' responsibility then to take care of themselves first, and develop a positive and healthy outlook on life.

Second, everyone in the family is expected to affirm and support other family members. The all too typical arrangement where the mother alone serves as the emotional support system within the family does not work well. When there are two parents in the family, both need to provide their share of nurturing, approval, and support, each in his or her unique way. For that matter, the children can also be supportive toward the parents, as well as toward each other. A parent who starts a new job, for example, may be in need of support just as much as the child who goes to a new school.

Third, the family understands that support does not include pressuring the person to do more, be better, or to be someone they are not. Some family members need to be encouraged to try harder, while others may need to be convinced to slow down and be easier on themselves. Being supportive means truly having the other person's best interests at heart. It is more supportive, and certainly healthier for the person, to help them accept realistic limitations than to set themselves up to fail.

Fourth, the family's basic mood is positive, based on hope and optimism. Problems and stresses are viewed as temporary and solvable. There is a team spirit and a sense that, as long as we have each other, anything can be overcome and things will work out.

Fifth, the family supports social institutions, but not blindly or automatically. Children are taught respect for institutions such as schools and places of worship, and the individuals who run them are treated respectfully. However, when there is a conflict between an adult and child it is important to also let the child explain his side of the story. The parents can check out the situation and determine where the problem lies. Sometimes the adult in a position of authority may indeed be the one who is being unfair or unreasonable. The child who is listened to and shown consideration for her feelings and opinions is given a powerful message about being accepted and valued.

---

5 Traits of a Supportive Family

- Parental Self-esteem
- Members Support Each Other
- Acceptance of Individual Limitations
- Positive, Optimistic Mood
- Discriminate Respect for Community Groups

The Lifelong Journey

Self-esteem is a complex phenomenon that is influenced by many factors and evolves over time. It is not something that can be taught, but rather is something that develops as an integral part of an individual's personality. All caring parents want their children to have high self-esteem, of course. While parents cannot exactly control that process, they certainly can have a good deal of influence over how it develops. The P.A.S. model (Perception, Achievement,

Support) of building self-esteem provides a framework parents can follow in helping children develop a healthy image, confidence, and emotional security. In particular, this model of self-esteem emphasizes the role of the family as an emotional support system that plays a crucial role in developing self-esteem.

It would be helpful to keep the long-term perspective in mind, namely that this process is ongoing and, realistically speaking, never ends. Self-esteem evolves as personality evolves, more rapidly in younger years but also fluid and changing to some degree throughout the person's lifetime. The goal of achieving a high level of self-esteem is not an endpoint or destination, but rather a journey. Help your children travel it as pleasantly and constructively as possible, even as you travel the same road yourself.

Chapter **12**

School Problems, Homework, and Other Headaches

Imagine having a job with a company that was spread out over six or seven different departments, which you have to report to every day. Imagine further that each department has a different boss, and they all assign you work to do on-site and take home without knowing how much work the other bosses gave. Most of those jobs are difficult, requiring a good deal of reading, writing, and memorizing. Most are not very interesting. The jobs require you to sit and listen all day, take notes, and remember what was said. You don't have your own office or desk, but have to keep track of papers and materials for each job. The worksite is usually crowded, noisy, and distracting. Your only break is a half hour lunch break, and the company cafeteria sells pretty bad food. How much would you enjoy this job? How good would you be at it?

DON'T IGNORE SCHOOL PROBLEMS, THEY MAY HAVE SERIOUS CAUSES

The "job description" above is an analogy used by psychologist Kathleen Nadeau, Ph.D., author of the book *Help4ADD@HighSchool*, to describe the life of a junior high school or high school student. It is not a job that most adults would relish, or hold for very long. The analogy above provides a reminder that receiving an education is a complex experience, fraught with its own challenges, frustrations, and disappointments. Society has changed in the past twenty years, and so have our schools. Many adults look back at their school years through a nostalgic haze and may recall a time of care-free innocence. Few of today's parents however can remember a time when their peers at school *wanted* to have more security guards in the hallways, searches for drugs, and metal detectors at the front door to prevent weapons from being brought in. To para-phrase the car commercial, this is *not* your father's high school. It is important for parents to be aware of the challenges and pressures their children face in schools today, communicate about them, and provide support when needed.

Children Are Natural Learners

We are all born curious and eager to learn. Children of all ages have a natural curiosity about the world. Watch even a very young child explore her world, getting into *everything* with relentless curiosity and energy. Limit the child in her activity or interrupt what she is doing, and get ready for a fuss or loud complaining. So what hap-pens when the children enter school, where their education becomes more structured and formal? Why does schoolwork become a chore for many children, and homework a major hassle or even a daily battle? The reasons are many, and it would not be fair to lay all the problems at the feet of schools or teachers. Children's ability to learn, the attitudes and roles of parents toward education, and the degree of cooperation between parents and teachers all play important roles.

Young children relate to the world through their senses. They are interested in things they can touch, see, smell, and taste. By the age of seven or eight, in first or second grade, children begin to deal more with verbal abstract concepts and show more interest in books and magazines. Some children are not ready in their intel-lectual maturation for the abstract verbal concepts they are expected to master in learning reading, writing, spelling, and math skills. Those children will struggle and become frustrated, particularly if any type of learning disability is involved. Some are simply not emotionally mature enough to handle the structure, rules, and responsibility of a classroom setting. Most children, however, can handle the demands of school capably, given sufficient supervision, encouragement, and help when they need it. Parents play a crucial role in their children's education, and can make the process easier or more difficult.

The Role of Parents in Children's Education

School success begins at home. Is the child emotionally secure and reasonably confident about his abilities? Is she comfortable in the knowledge that parents and family will help and support her in times of need? Is he prepared for the day, with all assignments completed and supplies in place, securely zippered inside the school bag? Did she have a good breakfast to start the day? If those questions are answered "yes," that child will be prepared for a productive day at school. If the answers are "no," chances are the parents have some work to do.

Children spend three-fourths of their time at home, even during the school year. This is where they first learn about responsibility, values, and goals. They learn how to get organized and work at a task by doing things at home. They learn how to recognize when they have a problem, communicate it to someone, and get help for it when they need assistance. They learn to respect other people's property, cooperate, and share. Children learn about following rules and respecting adult authority based largely on their relationships with their parents.

Respect for School   By the time the kids hit preschool, their parents will have either prepared them in these areas well, or not prepared them very well. The children's attitudes toward school will largely reflect the parents' attitudes, in positive or negative ways. If the parents respect the school's rules, teachers, and administrators, so will their children. If they stress the value of education, the children will hear the message and take it seriously. If the parents provide rules and realistic expectations about homework and study times, and enforce those rules, the children are much more likely to develop good work habits and take responsibility for the schoolwork. It can be tremendously helpful for both parents and children to help the child establish routines. A morning routine, homework routine, chores routine, and bedtime routine can be understood and followed by even young children.

The Parent-Teacher Partnership

Parents need to become partners with their child's teachers in order to help the school best meet their child's needs, identify and correct problems early on, and learn what they can do at home to help the child learn. A partnership implies a relationship based on cooperation and mutual respect, of course. Too often parents and teachers end up in a combative relationship over the nature of the child's problem, who is to "blame," and the appropriate solutions. Nobody benefits from these confrontations, certainly not the child. Sometimes the conflicts require mediation from a third party, such as the principal or school counselor.

Teachers Are Human Beings An outstanding teacher can make a positive impact on a child that lasts a lifetime. A bad teacher, or a teacher who is simply a bad match for a particular child, can also cause damage that may last a lifetime. It is the parents' responsibility to monitor how their child is getting along with the teacher, and to be aware of any problems that crop up. Having regular conversations with the child about how their day in school went, and occasional conferences with the teacher, should provide enough information.

The best teachers, as Dr. Kathleen Nadeau discusses in her book *Help4ADD@HighSchool,* are most likely those who show a genuine interest in their students, are able to be flexible and attentive to individual needs, are clear in their expectations and organized in their work, encourage rather than criticize when a child has difficulties, are excited about their job and enjoy teaching, and know the material well and can teach it creatively. Other teachers may fall so far short of these qualities that people wonder why they are employed as teachers. These teachers are more likely to be "going through the motions" rather than being involved with the children, are rigid and inflexible, use a cookie-cutter approach that is not sensitive to individual differences or needs, are unclear in what they expect, are disorganized, and try to motivate through shame and criticism rather than praise and encouragement.

Changing Teachers   If a parent discovers her child is struggling or having difficulties due to problems in the teacher-student relationship, then it may be appropriate to request a change in teachers. Many teachers will take offense at such a suggestion, but hopefully not if there is a valid problem and the child's interests are not being served. Before school administrators and teachers rise up in arms, let it be said that this option should be used very sparingly, and only as a last resort. The fact that a child does not "like" a particular teacher is not a reason in itself to change teachers or classrooms. If the teacher truly does not "like" the child, however, a change should probably be made in light of the potential for conflict and many negative messages the child might receive over the course of a year or a semester. Although this should not happen, some children are scapegoated by teachers who dislike them and may end up having a difficult, nightmarish year.

Defeating the Homework Gremlins

Few things in the history of modern parent-child relationships have caused as much strife as battles over doing homework or getting help with homework. As special educator Susan Setley writes in her very practical book, *Taming the Dragons: Real Help for Real School Problems,* helping with homework is not as simple as it sounds and "it can be a minefield." If a parent is sitting beside the child night after night, encouraging or threatening to coax more effort out of an unwilling and angry or frustrated child, or doing much of the homework for the child, then something is wrong. It is possible that the work is simply too difficult for that child, which may suggest some type of learning problem. In that case, an evaluation by the school psychologist or learning disabilities specialist might be very useful. Some children need more individualized help and intensive interventions at school, and if necessary, hiring a tutor to help with the homework. Oftentimes a high school or college student can make an excellent tutor. If a child has a significant weakness in an area that needs specialized kinds of help, a professional tutor might be required.

Establishing routines and a regular study time is usually a good idea. This provides some structure and order for the child, and also helps the parent to monitor how much time the child spends on homework and study. Teachers can provide a reasonable estimate of how long the homework should take to complete. Parents should consider where the best place is for the child to do homework. Some need privacy, and some do better sitting at the kitchen table with a parent nearby. The parent can encourage independence by being nearby but having something to do, such as reading a book, working on a crafts project, or paying the bills. Some children need quiet, while others *need* background noise such as soft music. Many disbelieving parents have ignored their child's insistence that "I study better with the stereo on." However, this may not be a case of the child being manipulative. Try it with the music on and off, and see which works better over time.

Arguments and Confrontations   These are destructive for everyone, and can turn into screaming matches between a frustrated adult and an angry and oppositional child. Again, having a routine in place, with reasonable rules that are consistently and calmly enforced, will help reduce the potential for confrontation. Sometimes one parent can work with the child on homework better than the other, or can work better on specific subjects. If a child needs more help than the parents can provide, consider hiring an outside tutor. If the child consistently fights against doing homework and shows indications of being overwhelmed, anxious, helpless, or simply stressed out, consider working with a child therapist. There may be emotional, behavioral, or learning problems that the child cannot manage without help.

Children with Special Needs: LD, ADHD, and Gifted

Even children with very high IQ scores can have problems with certain kinds of learning and academic work if they have a specific developmental disorder, also known as a learning disability (LD). These learning problems are often not apparent until a child enters school. As Setley notes in *Taming the Dragons: Real Help for Real School Problems,* there are three traits that are typical of students with learning disabilities. First, they have average intelligence or close to it, or even above average intelligence. Second, school achievement is significantly below expected levels in one or more specific areas, such as math, reading, or written expression. Based on their overall intelligence scores these students *look* like they should be able to handle grade-level math or reading work, for example, and their difficulties may be mistakenly attributed to lack of effort. Third, there is a pattern of significant differences among different areas of intellectual functioning that can explain the student's difficulties. It is very important that children with learning disabilities are diagnosed accurately and early in their academic careers. If a parent or teacher notices a child having significant problems in one or more specific areas of learning, an evaluation by the school psychologist might be a good idea.

Children with Learning Disabilities Need Special Attention, and Help   They are not lazy or uncaring children, but simply unable to master the tasks expected of them without getting the help they need. Children with learning disabilities have a much more difficult time moving from concrete learning to abstract learning. They may become very frustrated, flounder, fall behind other children, become discouraged, and stop trying. With the proper understanding and assistance, many children with LD problems do quite well. A child with poor auditory memory needs to have things written out, as well as hearing them. A child with poor visual processing skills needs to hear the information, discuss it with someone, and perhaps listen to it again on tape, in addition to seeing it on the blackboard and reading it in a book.

Parents also need to keep in mind that children develop at their own unique rate: some are early bloomers, some late. Some children talk well at eighteen months, some not until they are three years old. There are many instances of children who don't talk much at all until the age of three or four, but then start talking in complete sentences! These are natural differences in rates of development and do not indicate a learning problem. Differences in development of other cognitive abilities and many physical skills are also common. If there are concerns, a consultation with the child's pediatrician or teacher might help to clarify the situation.

Children with Attention Deficit Hyperactivity Disorders (ADHD)

Significant academic problems are also commonly seen among children with undiagnosed and untreated Attention Deficit Hyperactivity Disorder (ADHD). Contrary to the popular stereotype of a ten-year-old boy "bouncing off the walls," not all children with ADHD are hyper or disruptive. As many as a third of these children may simply have difficulty staying focused on the task at hand such as reading, doing written work, or listening to the teacher. Girls with ADHD in particular are not as overactive or hyper, and consequently their difficulties are more likely to be overlooked. In the past, professionals and educators wrongly believed that ADHD was much less common among girls than boys, precisely because the girls were less disruptive and drew less attention. The problems can be spotted in the children's behavior, such as having excessive difficulty completing work, being disorganized and forgetful, and often losing or forgetting assignments and supplies.

Undiagnosed and untreated LD or ADHD typically causes severe disruption in the child's ability to be productive and achieve at ability level. What greatly compounds the children's problems is when the LD or ADHD are not properly understood and the children are criticized and blamed for not caring or not trying hard enough. Many of them care very much and try very hard, but are simply spinning their wheels because they cannot achieve at a "normal" level without the proper help.

People With ADHD   Adults as well as children may have significant difficulties maintaining sustained focus and attention, jumping around from one idea to another or from one project to another, keeping track of things, and completing assignments or projects. For many people, there are also difficulties with memory as well, so that more frequent review is necessary. For some people, the attention difficulties are so bad that it makes it very difficult or impossible to read a book, for example, or even a chapter. People with ADHD in many cases need medication to help manage the biological symptoms of distractibility, impulsivity, restlessness, and other symptoms. It is crucial that treatment for ADHD also involves teaching the person behavioral skills to help them become better organized, set goals and manage time better, and become more consistent in their work. All of these behaviors play major roles in how productive and successful a person is going to be.

Children Who Are Gifted

Another group of children tend to have difficulty with the structured classroom environment, to the surprise and consternation of many parents and teachers. These are the very bright, gifted children who end up being bored, stifled, and unchallenged by the regular classroom work. The story of Kevin below illustrated the case of one very bright boy who, despite his best intentions, became labeled as a pain in the neck.

KEVIN'S STORY—A BRIGHT, DISRUPTIVE BOY

Kevin is a bright eight-year-old boy who fairly sparkles with energy and enthusiasm to learn. He developed a particular interest in geography, and collected six world atlases and three globes which he pored over and memorized. Which large city is also a country? Kevin could tell you that, and beam about it! He was very proud and anxious to show you what he had learned, at home and at school. While this child might seem like the dream student that any teacher would love to have in the classroom, such was not the case with Kevin and his second grade teacher, Miss Jones. He was constantly raising his hand in class when the teacher asked the students questions, and sharing his information with the children around him.

Miss Jones was initially pleased and impressed with his eagerness, but after a while considered Kevin's high level of participation to be unfair to the other students and stopped calling on him as often. This confused Kevin and frustrated him. He had the answers, why did the teacher ignore him? His frustration and competitiveness made passivity unbearable, and led to an impulsive blurting out of the answers even when the teacher refused to call on him. This understandably did not please the teacher, who viewed his new behavior as defiant as well as disruptive. A power struggle ensued, with Kevin losing five minute segments from his recess time for talking out of turn. The trouble was, he still could not help himself! This energetic and highly enthusiastic youngster was now being held back from recess, when he most needed to run around and expend some of his considerable energy and frustration. This attempted solution only compounded the problem and increased the frustration on all sides.

Not surprisingly, the disruptive behaviors continued, with Kevin becoming increasingly anxious and blurting out answers before he was being called on. On one particularly bad day he argued with

Miss Jones about the population of Malaysia, because he knew that he was right and would not concede to the teacher's request that he drop the subject. Kevin was also attempting to help the students around him when they had difficulty, even without being asked to do so. Miss Jones finally moved Kevin's seat to the very back of the room, where the children hung their coats, so that he would not be as disruptive to his classmates.

Kevin went home crestfallen that day, embarrassed about his punishment and confused about his teacher's exasperation with him. "She put me in the coat closet!" he complained to his parents. The baffled parents called Miss Jones the next day, and were surprised to learn that their bundle of enthusiasm, so loving and cooperative at home, was hell on wheels in the classroom. They simply did not recognize their child in the behaviors Miss Jones described, although they did not doubt her sincerity. After a conference between parents and teacher, it became clearer that he was very bored in class. A partial solution was to give him more challenging work on some assignments, and a special geography project to work on. Kevin would take one continent at a time and create color coded maps, showing the major cities, rivers, mountain ranges, and natural resources of each country. When he finished his work in class he was allowed to work on his project. An agreement was also made with Kevin that he might be called on to answer every fourth question from the teacher, maximum, but otherwise he had to give the other kids a chance to think about the questions and answer them themselves. This stopped being a problem, along with bothering those around him, when Kevin could occupy his time constructively with his project and not have to deal as much with boredom and frustration. Being able to run around at recess helped, too.

Schools Geared For Problems Our school systems are much more geared to providing services for the students having difficulties, who would fail without them, than for the bright students who may end up being frustrated by the very system that is supposed to help them develop their minds and learning capacities. There are concerns among some educators that providing special upper-level classes for students with exceptional abilities in certain areas would increase competitiveness, make children feel more pressured to succeed, and undermine the self-esteem of the majority of children who would not qualify for such classes. Others claim these concerns are misguided. We make it possible for the most talented students to develop their skills and shine in sports, the arts, and other extracurricular activities. Why not give them the opportunity to grow and shine in the academic areas as well? The fundamental value system of our society is based on opportunity, diversity, making choices, and meeting challenges.

Nurturing Special Skills   Although few people are "gifted" across the board, many of us have exceptional talents and abilities in one or more areas. These may include math skills, musical talent, writing ability, an eye for graphics design, and so on. A good argument can be made for giving those students every opportunity to develop their abilities in higher-level advanced classes, to whatever levels of achievement they are willing to strive for. Neither the needs of individuals, nor those of society, are met by limiting how much students can learn due to efforts to appeal to the lowest common denominator or to "dumbing down" the school curriculum.

Now for a word to parents: please *do not* push your children into classes or programs they do not belong in, or push them to try and achieve past their ability levels. This is a real concern for many knowledgeable, caring professionals in the schools who see the damage to the children that overzealous parents can cause by pushing their children too far. If parents try and push their children into accelerated programs when the children are not capable of performing at that level, they are setting up the child to fail and creating conflicts between themselves and the educators. This is a problem of bad parenting, not an educational problem. The role of the educational system should be to best meet the realistic needs of all students, whether learning disabled, of average ability, or gifted.

Chapter **13**

Create Shared Values and a Family Identity

A family is more than a group of people living together, sharing resources and responsibilities. Roommates sharing a house can accomplish those goals, or people living in a commune, yet these people may have no sense of kinship or family. A family provides, among other things, a sense of belonging and shared identity that extends beyond the individual. This involves a shared history and heritage that is passed along from generation to generation. The family history goes back hundreds of years sometimes, is repeated at family gatherings, and taught to the younger members. The family provides continuity between ancestors in the past, family members in the present, and future additions to the family as children are born or adopted. When adults join the extended family through marriage, they learn the family history. Every close knit family has a sense of "this is who we are," and the sense of identity that defines the "we" is uniquely theirs.

DON'T NEGLECT FAMILY TRADITIONS

The shared sense of identity makes it possible for the family to serve as a base, a place of belonging and support to be counted on and called upon when a family member is in need. The poet Robert Frost had by far the best definition of what a home is: "Home is the place where, when you have to go there, they have to take you in."

The sense of security that comes from having an accepting and loving family cannot be overestimated, nor duplicated elsewhere. Large amounts of money can buy lavish houses, even castles on mountaintops, but only a family can provide a home. The family may include two people or ten, may include children who come from different backgrounds through remarriage or adoption, and may include grandparents or other relatives, but the common bond of being part of the family unites everyone and strengthens everyone. Nurturing and maintaining the values and traditions that create the family identity is the process that holds it all together.

Strong Families Have Shared Values

Every family needs to answer the basic question: What is this family about? What do we believe in, value, hope to achieve? What do we oppose, dislike, strive to avoid? Each family develops a set of values and expectations that answers those questions and helps to define who "we" are. In this family we like one other and stand up for each other, no matter what. In this family we are Democrats, go into teaching or law enforcement careers, and hate racism. In this family we follow Jewish traditions, marry within our faith, and value high educational achievement. In this family we like to be physically active, get involved in sports activities, and go skiing every Christmas vacation. In this family we go to church every Sunday, value service to others, and respect and cherish our elders. In this family we tell stories about our grandparents who came over from Ireland, and have a large family dinner every St. Patrick's Day. It does not matter so much what specifically gives a family its own unique feel or look, as long as those qualities, values, and behaviors are understood and accepted by the members of that family.

Families that lack a set of core values or sense of purpose are more likely to become a collection of self-centered individuals, rather than a close-knit group that is supportive and emotionally close. People are likely under those circumstances to become focused primarily on selfish needs, with less emphasis placed on group affiliation or responsibility. Self-centered behavior often gets translated into becoming very materialistic or excessively achievement oriented. They may find themselves searching for happiness through bigger, fancier, and increasingly more expensive possessions, working relentlessly for the next promotion and higher job status, or an endless array of recreational activities. The lessons often learned are that buying things does not bring happiness when what is missing is much more fundamental: a deeper sense of meaning, purpose in life, and emotional satisfaction. Money never did buy happiness.

Family Traditions

Rituals, stories, colorful characters, memorable events, food, music, humor and jokes, all can become part of a family's traditions and shared identity. Part of this information is communicated verbally from the elder family members to the younger ones. In a variety of ways, however, a family lives out its traditions through its behavior. Family rituals are very important to a sense of cohesion and belonging. What gives them meaning is that they are performed with people we care about, which gives them heightened importance and provides for emotional satisfaction.

A family Fourth of July volleyball party that becomes an annual tradition is not simply a volleyball game and barbecue. It transcends sport and food and becomes a bonding experience, an opportunity to see the extended family, catch up on happenings, and share the camaraderie that cannot be found at any other volleyball party in the world. Opening Christmas presents first thing on Christmas Day, then driving over to grandma's house for breakfast, becomes a comfortable routine for children, parents, and grandparents. Listening to grandpa's corny jokes and taking home a large box of grandma's sugar cookies may also become part of the tradition. Planning and shopping for Halloween costumes, making handmade birthday cards, raking and bagging the leaves in the backyard together, and renting movies on Friday nights can all become a part of what this family does on a regular basis. What other families do is their business, but this is who "we" are.

Sharing Stories   Part of family tradition is also sharing stories about family members, both past and present. Each family has its share of colorful characters, heroes, saintly figures, rogues, or downright crooks, people who achieved something important, and those who suffered great calamities. Every family has someone who became famous or semi-famous, someone who became a black sheep, and someone who probably should have been locked away in the attic if that was not immoral and illegal. The history of most families is richer than any novel, and more beloved because it is *our* history. Repeating favorite stories about people and events is an enjoyable pastime at many large family gatherings. Whether the stories are told for their humor or entertainment value, or as morality tales, they serve to draw people together under the common umbrella of shared kin and shared history. The person in the story may have been a fool, and don't you dare follow his example, but at least he was *our* fool which affords him a degree of sympathy and even affection.

Rituals   These provide a sense of stability, which in turn provides security. This need may be more important now than ever, in our rapidly changing and mobile society. People move hundreds or thousands of miles away to pursue education, jobs, or for health reasons. Members of families that are close often find a need to stay in contact regularly, by phone, letters, or these days by E-mail. The emotional benefits are derived from staying in touch with the base, the loved ones, and thus maintaining one's sense of belonging within the larger group. By maintaining traditions and rituals within one's own family, it carries on the family spirit and maintains the family identity no matter what part of the country or world a family moves to. Traditions and rituals automatically convey a sense of common purpose and identity, and provide a sense of continuity and stability.

The Passing On of Traditions   This is very important to everyone in the family, whatever their age, status, or role. Older family members tend to see the value of traditions more clearly and to emphasize their teaching and preservation. Children enjoy traditions for their own sake, for the familiarity and stability they convey. Teenagers may rebel and pull away from traditions or rituals for awhile, as part of separating from the parents and developing their own sense of identity. This does not imply that adolescents get no benefit or enjoyment from traditional family activities, however, and they should not be excluded from them. Complaining about one more stupid Thanksgiving dinner at Aunt Harriet's does not preclude the turkey and pumpkin pie from still tasting good. Even the most rebellious teens find themselves appreciating and returning to family traditions more as they get older.

Ethnic, Racial, and Religious Traditions

In our multicultural, multiracial society, ethnic and racial backgrounds often provide a very important part in shaping family identity. Language, foods, dress, holidays, and other rituals may all be heavily influenced by ethnic and racial identity. Black, Hispanic, Asian, and other racial groups preserve and teach their respective racial heritage and traditions to children and base a great deal of family life around them. Even courtship, marriage rituals, and childrearing practices may be strongly influenced by ethnicity, particularly in the case of newly arrived immigrants. These diverse backgrounds provide a rich source of tradition and history, and need to be respected and maintained for the sake of communities, families, and individuals. This country has benefited from diversity since its inception, and will continue to benefit from it.

Religion plays an intricate part in the lives of individuals and families. For many people, religious beliefs provide meaning in life and a sense of purpose, as they have done for thousands of years. Religious beliefs can also provide a core of values that forms the value structure for families. Indeed, for many families religious values and family values are one and the same. By emphasizing higher values, religious values play a part in transcending the self and getting beyond selfish needs. By emphasizing service to others, many religions help to build a sense of community that extends beyond the family. Many family rituals are derived from religious beliefs and practices, and are taught from a very young age. Saying grace before a meal, for example, can be learned and practiced even by a three-year-old. These traditions all enhance the development of a sense of shared experience and belonging, of being part of a larger whole that strengthens the individual.

Family Reunions and Renewals

Close families do things together within the immediate family, and gather together within the extended family. People enjoy being with each other, and the nature of the occasion may be secondary to simply getting together. Holidays have in large part become rituals and family events, particularly the religious holidays. In addition to those holidays, birthdays, weddings, anniversaries, and funerals are occasions for the tribe to gather round each other. When families are split apart due to job moves and other causes, a planned family reunion may be what brings everyone together. These tend to be elaborate and expensive events that take a good deal of work and planning, and thus may not be held very often. When families remain emotionally close however, few things in life can match the warmth and joy of a large family reunion. The family members from near and far are drawn back to the family as a source of emotional nourishment and shared identity. The family remains a base for a lifetime, from cradle to grave.

Chapter **14**

Violence, Sex, Advertising, and Media Influence

The mass media of even thirty years ago—television, magazines, movies, radio, along with the new phenomenon of the Internet—is primitive compared to the media of today. The amount of information transmitted over the airwaves, cable wires, and in our mailboxes can be overwhelming. News, crises, entertainment, and commercials are pumped out twenty-four hours a day, seven days a week. A constant bombardment of advertising drives (and indeed creates) a need for goods and services. Violence is pervasive, on the news, in TV shows, movies, music lyrics, even children's cartoons. Turn on the news and you are hit with the latest tragedy from somewhere in the world, usually with footage caught on videotape and beamed via satellite to TV stations worldwide. Sexual imagery is everywhere, in entertainment and commerce, and used quite effectively commercially to grab attention, entice, and sell.

DON'T LET MEDIA MESSAGES DISTORT YOUR CHILD'S THINKING

Along with the sheer volume of information, there has been a tremendous increase in the intensity and graphic nature of information being presented to the public. The violence is more graphic, accepted, even celebrated in many movies and some types of popular music. What was once only suggested in terms of sexual images and behaviors in movies and on TV is now blatant and commonplace in popular forms of entertainment. To the surprise, indeed the utter shock and disgust of many parents, any young child with access to the Internet can find the most graphic, vulgar, pornographic material that their parents never imagined existed. All that is required is a computer, an Internet access account, and the basic knowledge of how to do a topic search. This topic will be covered below in the section on sex and the Internet.

Information Overkill

The effects of information overkill, in terms of sheer volume and intensity, is that our lives have speeded up in almost all areas. There is scarcely time to rest, relax, socialize, and catch one's breath. The incidence of stress-related disorders are up, such as high blood pressure, heart disease, anxiety, and substance abuse. Depression is more common, and is affecting children at younger ages. Children are feeling more stress as well, along with something less obvious but perhaps even more profound. Children are forced to grow up faster. The innocence of childhood is lost earlier, and there is not much time to be a child in a speeded-up world.

Defining Who We Are Through Media Images

Electronic and print commercial messages are highly visible and very sophisticated in their ability to create demands and to sell to meet those demands. The influence of the commercial media is not limited by any means to selling goods, however. The most powerful effect comes from the ability to create images of how people should look, dress, and behave. We all internalize some ideals of beauty, glamour, sophistication, and desirability that are portrayed in the media. No one has to twist our arms for this to happen, we do so willingly in the process of being entertained and amused.

The best marketing campaigns don't use a hard sell, but rather create an image that people want to emulate. If you want to "Be Like Mike," then you wear Michael Jordan's shoes, drink his soft drink, and when you get older perhaps wear his cologne and drive his sports utility vehicle. All of those things will not *make* you Michael Jordan of course, but if deep inside you can identify with the sports superstar even a little bit there is some sense of satisfaction in that. The point here is not to criticize Mr. Jordan, who in many ways has been an exemplary positive role model for young people. The point to consider rather is that media images and commercial messages are powerful influences that help to shape people's perceptions, desires, and behaviors. Unlike Michael Jordan's media image, some of what is internalized by our young people is decidedly negative, harmful, and unhealthy.

Media Images of Women   These can be particularly harmful for young girls when those images become distorted and unrealistic. Slenderness and fashion have become major preoccupations for girls and women, exaggerated to an unhealthy degree. Many will agree that something is wrong when "high fashion" for women is represented by models who look like anorexic heroin addicts. The diet industry involves hundreds of millions of dollars spent on foods, drinks, pills, and other potions as people quest relentlessly for thinness. Diet and weight-loss books are best sellers, never mind that many are harmful to health and useless in maintaining a healthy weight. Exercise spas and weight-loss clinics, and clubs and enrollment programs at gyms are a booming business.

Beyond striving for a certain body image, people also judge their worth and competence based on their looks. Others judge them in the same manner. Success is associated with slimness, while overweight people frequently face discrimination and criticism from others who unfairly assume they are lazy, messy, and lack character or self-restraint. These body image issues apply to both genders, but play a larger role in the lives and psyches of women.

The impact of a negative body image on a girl's life can easily affect self-esteem, relationships, and even physical health. Girls who don't "fit" the ideal image are prone to suffer low self-esteem, waste their time and mental energy obsessing over their looks, and refrain from doing things they might enjoy simply because they don't like how they look and may assume that other people perceive them in the same "bad" ways. It is always sad to see girls try to hide their bodies and beauty by wearing clothing too warm, too baggy, and too drab.

Dissatisfaction with their looks leaves many girls and women vulnerable to unsafe and dramatic attempts to change their bodies, and prone to developing eating disorders. While there is an increase in the prevalence of males with eating disorders, the majority with these problems is female. Eating disorders typically develop during adolescence. They are connected in a fundamental way to the identities people develop, which of course is highly subject to social and cultural influences. Women in particular have been under pressure to identify their sense of identity with their body shape and to modify their appearance for the sake of others.

Eating Disorders   Seven out of ten high school girls are unhappy with their bodies and want to lose weight. Even among female adolescents of *normal* weight, eight out of ten want to lose weight. Eating disorders, especially anorexia nervosa and bulimia, affect 10 to 15 percent of adolescent girls. Eating disorders are life-threatening and need to be identified and treated as soon as possible. The fundamental features of an eating disorder are an irrational fear of fat, very strong desire to become slender, and dissatisfaction with one's body, often coupled with a distorted perception of body shape. Unhealthy and dangerous weight management practices may include a semistarvation food regimen, self-induced vomiting, use of laxatives and diuretics, and excessive exercising. All of these harmful, dangerous behaviors are followed willingly (indeed, compulsively) by girls and women trying too hard to live up to a cultural image of who they should be and what they should look like.

Many women have rebelled against these cultural pressures, but many others still fall victim to them at the cost of their self-esteem, physical health, and sometimes their very lives. The upwardly mobile, status conscious young woman is caught in a crossfire of conflicting messages about the body and femininity. On the one hand she is encouraged to be an independent, career-oriented achiever who will leave behind the vulnerability and dependency represented by old notions of femininity. On the other hand she is still expected to work hard to develop relationships with men, be attractive to men, and live up to cultural images of femininity that are largely media driven. Which is the greater value, independence or conformity? The pressures to conform can be very powerful, and to adolescents dealing with the normal processes of developing a sense of self, they can feel overwhelming.

Violence and the Media

There is no question that movies, television, and music lyrics use more images of violence compared with twenty or thirty years ago. While much of the concern surrounding media violence and its effect on children has emphasized the role of the entertainment media, psychological research indicates that violence on television news is also the cause of significant fear in children. TV news violence instills fear and anxiety, to some degree in adults but most profoundly in children. A school shooting in Arkansas gets wide publicity nationwide, with the result that a child in Maine or Hawaii may well develop fears of being hurt or even killed at school. Televised damage from a tornado hundreds of miles away may well generate fears and even phobic anxiety about bad weather for children even in areas where tornadoes are uncommon. How many local news shows in large cities, and even in smaller communities, begin with the ominous words "There's been a shooting . . ."? Those types of violent stories tend to be the lead stories in local news shows because they are almost guaranteed to draw interest and attention and "hook" people into watching the show.

Violence on Television   According to research presented by the American Psychological Association, this definitely affects children negatively. Seeing violence on television produces three major affects on children. First, children may become less sensitive to the pain and suffering of others. Second, children may be more fearful of the world around them. Third, children may be more likely to behave in aggressive ways toward others. Studies at the University of Pennsylvania have shown that children's television shows contain about twenty violent acts each hour. Furthermore, children who watch a lot of television are more likely to think that the world is a dangerous place. Keeping in mind that children remember best what they see as opposed to what they hear or read, this is not surprising. The visual images of violence that children see on television on a daily basis make a powerful impression and stay with them for a long time.

Other studies have shown that children often behave differently after they've been watching violent programs on television. In one study done at Pennsylvania State University, about 100 preschool children were observed both before and after watching television. Some watched cartoons that had many aggressive and violent acts; others watched shows that didn't have any kind of violence. The researchers found that children who watched the violent shows were more likely to strike out at playmates, argue, disobey authority, and were less willing to wait for things than those children who watched nonviolent programs.

In other studies at the University of Illinois, it was found that children who watched many hours of television violence when they were in elementary school tended to also show a higher level of aggressive behavior when they became teenagers. By observing these youngsters until they were thirty years old, researchers found that the ones who'd watched a lot of television violence when they were eight years old were more likely to be arrested and prosecuted for criminal acts as adults. These findings provide clear indications that parents need to monitor the amount and the content of their children's TV viewing, particularly when children are young. There is also an implied need for the television networks to limit the amounts of violence shown in their programs.

Aggressive Girls   Television violence impacts girls as well as boys. A study conducted by the University of Michigan's Institute for Social Research showed that young girls who often watched shows featuring aggressive heroines in the 1970s (such as "Charlie's Angels," "Wonder Woman," and "The Bionic Woman") grew up to be more aggressive adults involved in more confrontations, shoving matches, chokings, and knife fights than women who had watched few or none of these shows.

The Power of TV   Researchers tell us that ages six to eight are very delicate and critical years in the development of children. Youngsters are learning "scripts" for social behavior that will last them throughout their life. Watching violent behaviors, whether on TV, in one's community, or in one's home, teaches children to use violent behavior when they encounter problems and conflicts in their lives. These behaviors may not show up right away, but will emerge many years later.

The television industry bears some responsibility for limiting the amounts of violence children are subjected to in television programming. In 1998, the television industry took steps toward implementing a ratings system for its programming that will give parents an indication of content not suitable for children. Unlike the Motion Picture Association of America, which uses an independent third-party board to rate films, television networks will rate their own programs. This seems like a positive step because, as Dorothy Cantor, Psy. D., president of the American Psychological

Association, notes: "We live in an era where both parents are often working and children have more unsupervised time. Parents need help in monitoring the amount of television and the quality of what kids watch while they're young."

The television industry also needs to provide that help for parents by curtailing the amount and intensity of violence depicted in all types of TV programs, and providing more content suitable for children. The history of the industry has not been exemplary in that regard, as demonstrated by experiences with the Children's Television Act. Congress implemented the Children's Television Act of 1990 to ensure that broadcasters provide "a reasonable amount" of educational content in children's shows. Researchers examined children's programming reports that came from stations who submitted license renewal files to the Federal Communications Commission (FCC), and found that broadcasters reported an average of 3.4 hours per week of educational programming that specifically was designed for children. A closer look at the programming however revealed that much of the content consisted of re-labeling old shows, such as Teenage Mutant Ninja Turtles and Yogi Bear, as "educational" shows. In reality, less than half an hour per day of educational programming was truly "educational" in nature. In response to those findings, the FCC tightened its definition of educational programming and established a three-hour-per-week requirement that took affect in 1997. It remains in the best interests of parents, however, to monitor the shows their children watch.

What Can Parents Do   According to the American Psychological Association, to further protect their children from the damaging effects of excessive violence in the media, parents can maintain some control in shaping their child's viewing habits by doing some or all of the following. Watch at least one episode of the programs your child watches so you can understand the content and discuss it with them. Discuss alternatives to violent behavior as ways to solve problems. Limit or ban programs that are too violent. Restrict television viewing to educational programming and other shows you consider acceptable. Encourage children to participate in other activities such as sports, hobbies, or playing with friends. Finally, limit the amount of time children spend watching television.

Sex, the Media, and the Internet

Sex sells. Marketers and promoters have known this for a long time and have learned to use it very effectively. There are few television shows that don't feature a major character, sometimes male but usually female, whose role is basically that of a sex object. This applies to adventure shows, comedy shows, soap operas, even many game shows. The soap opera genre in particular is being viewed by some as having been transformed into the equivalent of soft-core pornography. Music videos are rife with sexual imagery and scantily clad models or dancers. Music CD and cassette tape covers feature near nudity. Music lyrics have few boundaries.

Magazine ads sell clothes and sex, perfume and sex, cars and sex, cigarettes and sex. An area that has become highly sexualized is one that many parents are still unfamiliar with, and that is the burgeoning Internet. Adult-oriented magazines and movies are regulated at least, and not made easily available to minors. No such safeguards exist on the Internet, which is one of its defining features. Anyone with a computer, modem, and Internet access can get online and "cruise the net." The other defining feature of the Internet is that cyberspace is limitless, without boundaries, theoretically capable of being expanded forever. There are no limits to how large the content base of the Internet can grow.

Porno on the Net The amount of pornographic material currently found on the Internet is far beyond what most people suspect. In all honesty, it shocked this author, who is computer savvy and a veteran of online research and communication for many years. As an experiment we did an Internet search using a search engine and the content word "sex." Any child with basic computer skills is capable of doing the same. The results of such a topic search provides a list of Web sites that fit under that category, along with a link that can be clicked on to connect you automatically with that Web site. Typing in the keyword "sex" produced a list of an astounding *678,992 links!* Only the first fifty of these were examined by title and capsule description, and all fifty were links to pornographic Web sites. Using the keyword "porno" produced a smaller but still astonishing list of 86,031 links. Typing in the infamous four-letter "f" word, which many children curious about "dirty words" will do, produced a list of 130,045 links. All that is required to get connected to one of those sites is to click on their link.

These pornographic Web sites are not of the Playboy variety, featuring nude models leaning against sports cars. The majority feature very graphic, hard-core, often vulgar content that used to be limited to only the seediest adult bookstores. This is a new place to gather for fans of sexual fetishes, bestiality, sadism and masochism, sexual torture, and every conceivable perversion. Typical descriptions for the Web sites include "bizarre kinky sex peep show," "hottest adult entertainment and sex," and "fantasy porn." Typical names for the Web sites include Adult Playground, Mega Hardcore, and Naked Girlfriend Collection. One link led to a house of prostitution, and another to an agency that billed itself as "Israel's escort service." Keep in mind that the Internet is worldwide, and a number of the Web sites were in German, Dutch, Spanish, and French. Internet pornography respects no borders and few boundaries.

With the Click of a Button   The majority of the pornographic Web sites are "paid" sites, meaning they charge a fee to use their content. However, most sites appear to offer free "samples" that are very explicit and graphic. Any person, of any age, who clicks on a link to one of these Web sites gains access to very hard-core pornography samples. The only "safeguard" is a ludicrous warning that persons under eighteen years of age are not allowed to enter the Web site, followed by a question of whether the person is eighteen or older and agrees to view pornographic material. If you click the "No" button, you don't proceed any further. If you click the "Yes" button, you are admitted into the Web site to view the hard-core "samples." Keep in mind that neither the computer, nor the Web site, has any idea if the person clicking that "Yes" button is twenty-one, eighteen, fifteen, or ten years old. It is that simple, alarming, and sickening.

Parents who provide their children with computer and online access need to monitor their children's Internet use. The Internet is a vast, fascinating collection of all types of beneficial and educational materials. Universities, museums, historical societies, science agencies, zoos, and even your local school may have its own Internet Web site. The task for parents and guardians is to protect children from harmful, dangerous, and truly sick material which is not appropriate for children of any age. There are various types of software that can be programmed to help screen out pornographic Web sites, but of course nothing is foolproof. Some online services such as America Online provide parents the option to set up a "screen name" for their child and deny that account Internet access or the ability to view pictures. However, the best control is still parental supervision and involvement.

Bringing Kids Back Down to Earth

The media is making our kids grow up too fast, and striving to be things they cannot be or should not be. One mother of a fourteen-year-old girl describes with some dismay the influence of media images on her daughter. Like many other girls, her daughter internalized the female "ideal" as shown by TV shows, magazines, advertising, and music lyrics. "She studied *how* women looked, how they dressed, carried themselves, acted in their relationships. Of course, on TV, most female actresses are skinny, attractive, and often portrayed as bimbolike sex objects." Trying to live up to expectations of these media images is a losing proposition for "normal" children and teens. Beyond that, the children come to see the unusual, inappropriate, and unhealthy as part of everyday life. The kids become desensitized and jaded. "What bothers me," the mother continues, "is that the media is so saturated with graphic sex, violence, and drug use that it has become an everyday thing. *Nothing* raises an eyebrow for her! When she was eleven my daughter was discussing oral sex like it was some ordinary everyday topic of conversation."

What Can Parents Do?   Start with two fundamental things, setting limits and encouraging communication. In terms of limits, parents need to monitor the amount of television watching and the type and quality of programs their children watch. Begin that at a young age, and it will become part of the family culture and routine. Although we live in a time where both parents are often working and are more lax in their supervision, rules and expectations still need to be set and enforced regarding television shows, movies, magazines, music CDs, and so on. Programs or materials that are inappropriate for children need to be off limits. Other activities need to be encouraged and pursued when possible. No child, or adult, needs to be a slave to the electronic, addictive monster in the family room.

Second, parents can discuss the media influences with their children and share their own views and values. It can be made clear that news stories often lead off with violent or tragic stories, but that does not mean that life in general is violent or tragic, and news shows should not instill fear in children. One does not have to have the latest video game or the most expensive shoes to be "cool." The "glamour" magazines often present artificial and unhealthy stereotypes, and no one has to strive to live up to ridiculous images. Commercials and ads are used to persuade you to buy things, and many of them are pretty silly. Does anyone really need to buy all that useless junk? Keep an open dialogue going with your children and communicate, communicate, communicate.

Set Those Limits!   There is a very good chance that you won't be very popular with your children when you limit their access to the media. You will hear that all their friends watch the TV show that you consider obnoxious, and everyone else has the video game where people's heads get torn off and blood and guts spill out. How can *you* be so unfair? The issues for parents is one of popularity or responsibility. The parents' job is to protect the child from harmful influences, no matter if the child agrees or objects. If you share your values, concerns, and love with the child, most children will accept the limits even if they don't like them. And if they don't accept them, the parents job is to enforce them anyway. Acting in the child's best interests, and protecting them from harmful influences, is the greatest show of love. Buying your child the new version of Psycho Ninja Killer Blood Sport is indulgence.

Chapter **15**

Play, Laugh, Talk, Celebrate

"A good laugh is sunshine in a house."
—WILLIAM THACKERAY

A family is about relationships. The essence of a happy
marriage and close family, deep down at its core, includes
relationships that are accepting, loving, and emotionally
nurturing. Good family relationships are based on loving one
another, communicating with one another, and sharing our lives
emotionally as well as materially. A family that lacks these qualities
in the relationships among its members will not have a strong
sense of loyalty, security, or intimacy. A marital relationship that
lacks these qualities is most likely a troubled marriage.
Relationships require many things, develop over time, and are
built on shared experiences. A close family does not happen by
accident, but is shaped and nurtured by the attitudes and behaviors of the family members toward each other. A family cannot
grow and prosper unless its members make time for each other,
show interest in each other, and look after each other, day after day,
year after year.

TIME, THE PRECIOUS COMMODITY

The first requirement for creating close family relationships is spending time together. This seems so obvious and basic that it is often
taken for granted, yet how many families fail to pass this simple but

crucial test? Spending time together. The thought of it can be daunting to parents who are already pressured and stressed due to demands from careers, financial needs, demanding bosses, car pools, housework, and responsibilities to community organizations, schools, and places of worship. Who has time to relax and have fun anymore? The better question however might be, who can afford *not* to make time for relaxation and fun family activities?

Taking the Time for Intimacy

The process of developing intimacy and warm feelings involves talking, listening, communicating, and playing together. The family that does not have time, or *make time* for these activities, will find it difficult if not impossible to thrive as a family and meet the emotional needs of individuals within the family. Having a strong sense of family is not about which house you live in, where you shop, or what kind of car you drive. It is not about material things. Family unity does not depend on the Mercedes, the job promotion, the batting title in little league baseball, the diamond earrings, or the ski vacations in Vail. All of those things are nice to have of course, but are never enough by themselves to create emotional satisfaction and close family relationships. The overzealous pursuit of material possessions and personal accomplishments often leads to the opposite in fact, namely neglecting family relationships. Financial success and personal glory are worthy goals and can be achieved of course, but hopefully not at the expense of family time and family relationships.

Is there any family that is not, well, *busy*? "Lack of time might be the most pervasive enemy the healthy family has," Dolores Curran writes in *Traits of a Healthy Family*. If time is not managed well, parents and children end up running around like gerbils, constantly rushing from one activity to another. The hectic rush of activity is stressful in itself, but lack of opportunity to unwind and relax makes things worse. A stressful family is characterized, as

Curran notes, by a continued sense of hurry and urgency, underlying tension that causes many quarrels and fights, a preoccupation with escape and having time to oneself, constant frustration about not getting things done, a sense that time is going by too fast, and a nagging desire for a simpler life. All families experience periods of heightened activity and stress, of course. Ideally those periods are temporary. If the hectic activity becomes a way of life, the family is asking for trouble. Individuals cannot function well on a burnout schedule, and neither can families. Sooner or later something breaks down.

Taking the Time for Activities   If necessary, time for family activities must be scheduled, planned, and written down on the calendar, and regarded as sacred or holy to that family. There needs to be free, relaxed time for activities that are not rushed, competitive, or demanding on family members. This is when people can catch their collective breath and unwind. The nature of the activity does not matter as much as simply having the opportunity to be together. This planned family time must be set aside by the parents, as a conscious goal, despite the demands of work, friends, and other social institutions. It matters not if you play checkers, rent a movie, shoot baskets, or go out for ice cream. Value the family time and guard it fiercely, particularly when the children are young. Even teenagers need some free time to "chill out" and unwind, and they should be provided that opportunity.

Talk

One of the most common complaints heard in unhappy families is that "we don't communicate." What exactly does that mean? By our very nature as human beings people communicate all the time, verbally and nonverbally, in positive and negative ways. When one person yells at another, that is surely communication, which mostly sends the message that "I am angry with you." Turning a cold shoulder and avoiding or ignoring the person is another way of communicating, albeit seldom a constructive one. When people complain about lack of communication, it usually implies a failure to share intimate thoughts, needs, or feelings. "We are not communicating" is another way of saying "I am not being heard" or "my emotional needs are not being met." Chances are, that assessment is accurate.

Family Members Need to Talk with One Another, on a Regular Basis   This should be done about whatever subjects interest them or may need to be dealt with. Simply catching up on the day's events is a great way to show interest and share plans, concerns, goals, and feelings. Each member within the family needs to be heard and responded to. Each needs to feel that he or she has a place within the family, will be taken seriously, and will be provided with support when needed. At times scheduling a family meeting can be a big help, providing the opportunity for all to share their concerns and work out what needs to be done. Responsibilities can be assigned, conflicts discussed and resolved, and a stronger sense of unity and team spirit developed. Family meetings should be run as a democratic exercise, not a boardroom or business meeting.

A particularly good time for family discussion is during family meals. The value of eating meals together has unfortunately been overlooked and neglected in our fast-paced culture. The centuries old process of eating a family meal provides a golden opportunity to combine two pleasurable events, namely eating good food and spending time with people we care about. The needs of both nutrition and communication are satisfied. Ideally, meal times should be happy times, relaxed and casual. This is *not* a time to discuss problems, misbehaviors, homework assignments, or the tax return due next week. Mealtime conversation should be casual, democratic, and free spirited. Jokes, funny stories, and silly humor go equally well with salad, entrée, or dessert. This is a time when every family member has the freedom to be themselves, and takes joy in expressing whatever might be on their minds. Now *that* is communicating!

Play

Individuals who are obsessed with a high work ethic feel guilty about taking time off for play, recreational activities, or relaxation. They live a high-stress lifestyle that can easily become boring, unfulfilling, even depressing. This principle applies to families as well. Parents pass along their attitudes about work and relaxation to their children, and the family develops expectations about work and play. Families can develop habits of taking time off to play and relax, without feeling guilty about it, or they stay caught up in work and responsibilities and let the pressures and stress mount. Which attitude is more likely to build close family relationships?

Happy, close-knit families understand the need to get away from work and responsibilities. Parents understand the value of spending time together, and doing fun and relaxing things either as a group or individually. The family needs to make a habit of taking time to play, and enjoys that time without feeling guilty. There are times to play board games, video games, sports, work on puzzles, or simply pack a lunch and go on a picnic. Make time on weekends to play tennis, see a movie, or go fishing. Regular recreational activities become part of the schedule, such as an annual family volleyball game, basketball tournament, or ski trip. Even very young children can get involved in activities such as going sledding in winter, camping in summer, or just having a barbecue in the back yard. Families make time for and take vacations together, and indeed consider that sacred and precious time which is reserved only for them. Vacation time might involve siting on the beach for a week and reading, golf, tennis, biking, camping, or hiking. The nature of the activities don't matter as much as the fact that the family is spending time together and doing things they enjoy together.

No Money   One complaint some parents make is that "we don't have the money for recreational activities." This is a poor excuse. There are no fees or taxes on having fun! A backyard barbecue and basketball game involves the cost of the food. A summer afternoon at a public beach involves the cost of transportation, and a trip to the zoo or museum might involve very small admission fees. A picnic or a hike can be done very cheaply, again for the cost of transportation and a few packed sandwiches, fruit, and drinks. Take fifteen minutes before bedtime and play a game with the kids, or read to them. Motivated families in a financial pinch find inexpensive ways of having fun, and then pursue those activities with joy and enthusiasm.

Laugh

A family with a sense of humor is simply fun to be around. It's more relaxing and pleasant to be a member of that family! A good sense of humor helps keep things in perspective when the frustrations and disappointments of life pile up. Humor takes the "edge" off conflicts and disagreements, and can be very useful in defusing angry or potentially explosive situations. Children enjoy jokes and humor just as much as adults do, and in fact they are not all that picky about the quality of jokes they hear. Funny stories about someone's day, or something that happened to someone they know, all help to lighten the mood and keep more serious issues in perspective.

Parents help to set the tone about using humor and allowing silly behavior that is playful and hurts no one. This in turn helps establish an emotional tone for the entire family, whether it is somber or upbeat, serious or relaxed, freewheeling or strict. If the parents can laugh at themselves, and accept their mistakes and shortcomings, it sets a very important example for the children to be more accepting of themselves and not to overreact to their own foibles and mistakes. Playful parents tend to raise playful children. Worried, anxious, angry parents tend to raise children who are also anxious worriers. How do *you* want to approach life, and what do you want to teach your children?

Humor Is Important   It benefits emotional health by managing stress, frustration, and anger. It also has important benefits for one's physical health because it promotes relaxation and helps decrease stress. Grim, tense, humorless people are more prone to physical illnesses and get less enjoyment out of life. A good sense of humor improves the quality of family relationships and the general quality of life.

A distinction should be made between good-natured humor and hostile or critical humor. Laughing at jokes, stories, or even at one's own mistakes can be a very positive and healthy experience. Humor that shames someone, embarrasses, belittles, or ridicules is neither funny nor healthy. Making fun of someone's shortcomings or laughing at their failures in a way that ridicules the person is destructive and should not be acceptable behavior. What might be considered humorous by a comedian on stage who ridicules people in the audience may not be at all acceptable between family members. Humor should lighten the mood and lift people's spirits, not tear them down or make them unhappy. Making a cruel joke and saying "but I was only kidding!" does not make it all right, because hostile humor can cut deep. When children don't understand this distinction, parents need to teach it to them.

Celebrate Accomplishments and Milestones

Everyone's life has its share, or more, of frustrations and failures. It also has its share of accomplishments, achievements, and important milestones. Happy families make it a point to celebrate achievements and important events. Graduations, birthdays, completing important projects, winning a prize, job promotions, engagements, weddings, and births can all be reason enough to have some type of celebration and acknowledge the person or persons involved. Most people are not very good at giving themselves credit for their accomplishments, which makes it doubly important that family and friends help them acknowledge their successes and celebrate with them. Successes and victories taste even sweeter when they are shared with people we love.

Happy families easily find reasons to have a celebration. Many times this comes naturally from being involved in the activities and accomplishments of other family members. Achievements should be acknowledged and celebrated. Some have argued that praising children for their achievements will make them feel that they are only loved when they achieve, however, I find this notion rather silly. Children will feel loved if there is love in the family and it is communicated on a daily basis, in the ways that family members treat each other. Celebrating and praising achievements is only the cherry on top of the cake. Every person in the family can get his or her just due, whether that involves a birthday, a graduation, a promotion, athletic achievement, or having one's pet pig win a prize at the county fair. Acknowledge the person *and* the accomplishment, praise the effort, and celebrate!

Families Are Made of These

What do you remember as cherished "family times" when you look back on your childhood? Several adults were asked to respond to this question. The answers vary from person to person, and family to family. A common thread that emerges however is that people look back on times and activities when the family truly set aside time for each other and enjoyed a common activity. Those events, traditions, and rituals create a sense of family identity and help develop warm and close relationships. Some of the responses are printed below:

> We started having "Magical Mystery Tours" in the summer—
> everyone gathers in the car and we just . . . take off. We never
> know where we land for the day trip. At the last one, we ended up

trout fishing at a trout farm and picking raspberries on the way home. A new tradition that we'll continue, I'm sure.

With life as busy as it is, we cherish family vacations, and plan and protect them jealously. We go out of our way to engineer holidays to alluring places where no one we know will be there—just us. This way we have lots of time playing together; or just hanging out together on a beach, digging in the sand or watching the water. Time for talks and comfortable quiet time together.

After dinner in the summertime my dad would play the guitar out on the back porch and sing country songs. We would all gather around and sing with him. When my sister learned to play the guitar she played with him.

One of our traditions with our children was "talk about the day." When we were tucking them in, we would talk about the day. We made sure that when we left them for the night, the last discussion with them was about something *good* that had happened that day. But the "talk about the day" was something they loved. We'd say "I'll read you a story," and then they would say "And then 'talk about the day, right?'"

Barbecues, the ones that last into the night, past the kids bedtime. We all are tanned from the sun of that day, and the kids are filthy! . . . but filthy in a good way! They are covered with the dust and dirt from swinging on the swings and running barefoot all day long. Their cheeks are sticky from the roasted marshmallows, and the barbecue chicken that their dad has been cooking nonstop! We all go running around the yard catching fireflies. All of us trying to catch that elusive one with the green light on its tail! It's now too late for baths! So to the kids delight, I tell them a nighttime dip in the pool for all of us will suffice. After they are clean and shivering from the chill night air my husband and I wrap them in warm fluffy towels, take them inside, and put them in their pajamas. We tuck them into bed with their jars of fireflies blinking on their nightstands . . . yup! The green one got away again! They always say while we're kissing them good night "this was the best day ever!" And my husband and myself agree it always is!

Every Sunday night, my father would sizzle up a big batch of popcorn (we'd beg for Jiffy Pop), and the three of us kids would trail behind him as he marched into the den singing some old marching song. Then we'd settle in to watch "The Ed Sullivan Show," stuffing our faces.

As a child, my most cherished family times were on vacation. My dad was a lawyer and worked from early morning till late at night. Vacations were heaven. We did lots of things together at the seashore community we visited. Lots of crabs to catch, even a snapping turtle or two. My dad and I liked to surf fish (mostly I watched), and we talked. I think I liked piggyback rides and shoulder rides from my dad along the sandy lanes to the store to buy candy almost the best.

Every spring, around March or April, "The Wizard of Oz" would be shown on TV and it was a given that we'd all watch this as a family . . . well . . . all except my older, "hippie" brother.

Vacations to Florida with my kids to visit my parents where we all went to the local crab-house to celebrate grandpa's birthday and crack crabs on tables covered with newspaper. Playing board games and making soup, especially on snowy days when there was no school or on weekends. Jewish holidays at our parents with the kids where we ate things like matzo ball soup, stuffed cabbage, and brisket. Ball games with the kids to see dad play while we cheered.

On Sunday nights it was a tradition to watch the Walt Disney movie. We were not allowed to watch TV so this was a real treat. We also were not allowed to have ice cream or soft drinks and during this occasion we were allowed to have a "7-Up" or ice cream—or do a combo—a float!

Sunday morning brunches. Groaning about getting up, but feeling reassured to smell coffee, see bagels, lox, etc., and see how many family members stroll in. Watching the parade on Thanksgiving morning in robes and slippers, while the house starts to fill with fabulous smells. Saturday morning challenges to cleaning up one's bedrooms in unison . . . ready, set . . . GO! Saturday afternoon matinees at the movies . . . popcorn, drinks, and the shock of light upon leaving! Going sledding . . . more time spent dressing and undressing than in the cold!

I make a Chanukah party every year and when we light the candles, we make up the words to the holiday songs because I can never remember them. They get a big charge out of that. I act like a total nut-case, singing nonsense and dancing around the kitchen table. My husband takes videos of the insanity.

We go to Sanibel Island every winter—the kids refuse to switch destinations—and we all rent bikes and have a blast. I don't think I could even talk them into a Caribbean vacation at this point. My husband books a fishing trip each time and the kids all look forward to a day on the boat with their dad. I sit home and read!

In many cases the events described above were very simple things, but the warmth and intimacy of those experiences comes through even when people recall them many years later. Many of the experiences involved food, not surprisingly. A family event that combines physical nurturing with emotional nurturing, and entertainment fun thrown in, is very tough to beat! Some of the memories involved vacation time, when the family is isolated from everyday distractions and truly focused on each other. The defining features for those wonderful memories are time spent together, putting away responsibilities, doing something relaxing and fun, and enjoying time with each other. The family that can make these events a regular part of its lifestyle gets benefits from them that truly last a lifetime.

Chapter **16**

Hold Family Meetings

The need for parents to be in charge, to provide guidance and caring which serves the best interests of the child, does not imply that parents need to be dictators or autocratic rulers whose every word should be treated as gospel. Parents who are dictators are usually bullies. They may earn their child's fear and grudging obedience, but at the cost of losing the child's respect and affection. One of the ironies of parenthood is that we raise our children so that they grow up into responsible, independent adults who no longer need us for their survival and well-being. This involves teaching independent thinking, decision making, taking responsibility for oneself, and cooperation with others in the spirit of teamwork.

DON'T BE A DICTATOR, ENCOURAGE FAMILY DECISION MAKING

One of the best opportunities for family members to communicate and listen to each other in a cooperative way is during regular, scheduled family meetings. This is where ideas can be expressed freely in a democratic atmosphere, where the opinions of children and adults are heard and treated respectfully. Each family member is given equal opportunity to have their say. Parents can receive feedback from the children, set or modify rules, and delegate responsibilities.

Children are given more decision making opportunities during family meetings, which helps promote responsibility, self-discipline, and independence. Disagreements or conflicts are discussed and worked out as best as possible, but again in a spirit of cooperation and working toward common goals. The shared time together, focused on family needs and working cooperatively, also helps create a family bond and sense of unity.

Why Have a Family Meeting?

In their book *Raising a Responsible Child,* psychologists Don Dinkmeyer and Gary McKay define some of the general purposes of a family meeting. The meetings create a sense of belonging and acceptance. They encourage open and honest communication. They provide opportunity to agree on rules and plans, thus enhancing cooperation. They can help to resolve conflicts. The meeting is a time to discuss plans and upcoming events, and give updates on projects or activities family members are involved in.

Open discussion and dialogue allows for each family member to be heard. Children are involved in the decision making process, and everyone gets an equal vote on matters that are brought up for a vote. The family meetings should always be held in a spirit of cooperation and mutual respect, not as competition between family members or a power struggle. This is not the time to assert parental authority in the decision making process.

The Meeting Provides an Opportunity for Complaints   These should be aired during a period of relative calm and cooperation, rather than in the middle of a heated conflict. Not surprisingly, this makes it easier to reach compromises and find positive solutions to disagreements. Conflicts and complaints might even be deferred during the week if the participants agree to wait and deal with them during the family meeting. The meeting leader, or chairperson, needs to help keep the family focused on the problem being considered until some kind of solution or helpful compromise is reached. Solutions are easier to find, and usually easier to accept, if they are the product of a cooperative group effort as opposed to a ruling from one person in authority.

Making Family Meetings Run Smoothly

The structure and format for a meeting is up to each individual family. Certain tried and true principles have been found to be very helpful, however, and these should be kept in mind and perhaps experimented with to see what works best. A family meeting can be held once a week, or more often if needed. Emergency meetings can be called anytime a crisis develops, or some important matter needs tending to. This is a time for the family to band together, circle the wagons if need be, figure out problems, and agree on solutions.

A parent usually serves as the chairperson of the meeting, but children can be and indeed should be given opportunities to lead the meetings as well. The job of the leader is to start on time, give each person the opportunity to be heard, decide whose turn it is to speak, and help the family stick to a topic until some resolution has been reached to whatever problem is brought up.

Votes are taken to decide family decisions. Some matters cannot be left up to democratic rule of course, such as how much TV to watch or whether or not homework gets done, but many decisions can certainly be voted on. The meetings might last only fifteen minutes, an hour, or more. Attention should be given to the limited patience and ability of younger children to sit through an extended family discussion.

Decisions on privileges and allowances can also be made during the family meetings. The decisions and rules that come out of a meeting need to be enforced by the parents of course, as with any other family rules. Once a rule is established it needs to be respected and followed, unless modified or changed at another family meeting.

Chores, Curfews, and Responsibilities

Most parents do not find it useful to pay children for doing their chores; rather the chores should be done as part of the child's responsibility within the family. Making the child's allowance dependent on chores being done is pretty much the same as paying the child for the chores. For that matter, so is withdrawing a child's allowance if chores do *not* get done. If an allowance is given it should be given without any tie-ins to responsibilities, but simply as a way of providing spending money and giving the child an opportunity to learn how to manage money.

If incentives or consequences are needed to encourage a child to complete their chores and responsibilities, these are better tied in with freedoms and privileges. A child who is reluctant to clean his room on Saturday morning might be told that he cannot watch TV or use the phone until the room gets cleaned, for example. It is then up to the child to follow through and complete the chore in order to earn back those privileges.

Bedtimes and curfews should be discussed and set for each child. This is usually done on the basis of a child's age, with increasing freedom and privileges as the child matures.

Responsibilities for everyone in the family need to be discussed and assigned, including age appropriate responsibilities for the young children. Children are less likely to make a fuss about doing chores if they had a say in choosing what their areas of responsibility are. It is easier to build a spirit of cooperation by asking for volunteers for the various household tasks, when this is feasible. If there are no volunteers, the family members can decide who does what from a list of household chores. If there is a really unpleasant job, such as picking up the dog doo-doo in the backyard, family members can take turns doing those tasks so that everyone shares the pain.

Chapter **17**

The Brady Bunch Meets Cain and Abel

ere is a safe prediction: if you're a parent and you have more than one child, you're going to see sibling rivalry develop. It cannot be avoided, but with some work and practice it can be managed so it doesn't get out of control. Sometimes the rivalry is mild and only requires occasional intervention. If that's the case, then count your blessings and praise your kids for getting along so well with each other.

DON'T IGNORE OR OVERREACT TO SIBLING RIVALRY

With some children, the sibling rivalry gets so intense, angry, and hostile that conflicts happen several times a day. Some disagreements may escalate into physical aggression and violence. In that situation, forceful parental intervention may be necessary, and sometimes even professional intervention is needed in the form of counseling or family therapy. The rivalry may last a few years, or it can last a lifetime.

It's Normal, So Skip the Blame

Sibling rivalry is normal. Parents should not blame children for it when it happens, nor blame themselves for being "bad" parents because their children disagree and argue. The realistic goal is to help the children find ways to deal productively with jealousy, conflicts, and anger. Jealousy among siblings is very common, and often starts when the sibling is born. Babies get tons of attention because they require it, because they're adorable and cute, and because, let's face it, they're "new" to the family. Now imagine being the child who has suddenly been displaced as the center of his or her parents' attention. Some feelings of resentment, jealousy, and even anger are probably normal under the circumstances.

For parents who have difficulty understanding this, Adele Faber and Elaine Mazlish in their excellent book *Siblings Without Rivalry* bring up the metaphor of a spouse who brings home another spouse. Imagine being a wife whose husband tells you: "Honey, I love you so much that I've decided to bring home another wife just like you!" Or imagine being the husband, and your wife brings home a rival. How would it make you feel? How might it make you want to treat the "other" person, the one who is now competing for your loved one's time and attention? Now imagine dealing with those feelings when you're three years old, or five, or ten. Looked at in this way, it's clear that sibling rivalry is part of human nature. Children will compete and fight over property, attention, friends, space, and their parents' love. Younger children will compete to keep up with their older siblings, and the older ones may try to keep the younger siblings "in their place." The role of parents is not to eliminate this behavior, because in fact it would be asking children not to behave like children, but rather to keep it within tolerable limits.

The Lessons Learned When we look beyond the problems, it is important to recognize that sibling rivalry can also be a positive and constructive experience. Many parents might disagree with that—we can imagine heads shaking in bewilderment from coast to coast while reading the previous sentence! Consider however that many of the lessons and skills learned in clashing and competing with our siblings are valuable preparation for dealing with life's challenges. A direct result of dealing with our brothers and sisters while growing up is that we learn how to deal with others, work out disagreements, handle anger appropriately, deal with bullies, and appreciate the benefits of sharing and considerate behavior. This may not always be apparent when we watch the five-year-old trying to strangle the three-year-old for taking his blocks, but sibling rivalry does indeed produce some benefits.

What Parents Can Do

Once we can accept that sibling rivalry is real, common, and not going to go away, our responsibility as parents is to help manage it as best we can. Where to start? It's important to establish ground rules within the family for what is acceptable behavior, and what is not. It is the parents' responsibility to teach these rules and *keep* teaching them until the behavior sticks. Children as well as adults have certain basic needs that must be respected by everyone in the family. The need for privacy requires that people knock on the door before going into someone's room, for example. The need to respect other people's property requires that you ask first before using or borrowing someone's toys, clothes, CDs, or other property. It is important for everyone to express feelings respectfully, and to ask for favors nicely instead of making demands. Abuse is never okay, whether it be verbal or physical. Allowing disagreements or arguments to escalate into a physical confrontation is never okay. Enforcing these rules for everyone, children and parents both, will go a long way toward helping everyone in the family get along with each other, and will also help keep the sibling rivalries in check.

Children can often resolve their differences among themselves, particularly if the conflicts are over minor things. Sometimes the most helpful thing a parent can do is simply listen to both sides respectfully, express faith in the children's ability to find a solution, then leave the room. A common mistake for parents is to try and play Solomon, the wise and impartial dispenser of justice. This simply doesn't work and is almost guaranteed to leave one child feeling cheated or misunderstood. Similarly, it is not productive to try and find out whose fault it is, or where the blame lies. Any parent who has asked the question "who started it?" knows that this is not a useful question. The answer is always "he did" or "she did." That does not mean the children are lying to you; usually they're simply describing the situation from their own point of view. It is more helpful to focus them on finding a solution, rather than figuring out how the problem started.

When Anger Gets Physical

Sometimes intervention by adults is necessary, particularly if the conflicts escalate to physical aggression. At that point, the parents must step in and assert their parental authority. The children may need to be physically separated and each sent to a different room for a cooling-off period. After the anger has cooled off, then perhaps the problem can be discussed. Children should be permitted to express their feelings, indeed encouraged to do so, including feelings of anger, resentment, and so on. Feelings need to be expressed in appropriate ways, however. It is okay to express feelings with words, but not through behaviors such as hitting, punching, kicking, biting, throwing things, and so on. The "no fighting, no hurting" rule needs to be made very clear and then enforced consistently. Even very young children can understand this rule: people are not for hitting! Verbal expression of anger should not include name-calling or swearing. Children can understand this rule as well, although it may be difficult for them to follow in the middle of an argument. It is up to the parents to set the limits on what is allowed, and what is not. I know of one mother whose basic rule in dealing with her three sons' conflicts with each other is "no blood, no broken bones." Other parents will not even tolerate mild swearing or cuss words.

Opening Up Communication

The best ways for parents to handle conflicts among their children is to open up communication so that the children can solve the problems between themselves. Feelings need to be acknowledged and put into word, in order that both children can understand the emotional impact of their behavior. Positive feelings need to be acknowledged just as much as negative ones when the children are cooperating and getting along. Sometimes it is better to give feelings creative expression, which helps to clarify them and make them more "real" or tangible. Writing a letter to someone you're angry with helps to express frustration and hostility in a safe way, even though the letter is never given to the person. Making a list of the sibling's "faults" and discussing these with the parent, or drawing a picture of the person they're angry with, can also allow for safe expression of negative feelings. Giving helpful suggestions along with expressing feelings can be very constructive as well, and sets the stage for future cooperation. A statement of "you're a pest and I don't want you ever touching my stuff again" is not very constructive. It may be more productive to hear that "I don't like it when you take my CDs from my room, so ask me first if you want to borrow them."

Stages of Conflict   In their book *Siblings Without Rivalry,* Faber and Mazlish discuss stages of conflict which are common in sibling rivalry. Normal bickering can be ignored, even acknowledged as an experience that will teach the children conflict resolution skills. When the situation is heating up and adult intervention might be required, it can be very helpful to acknowledge their anger ("you two sound like you're mad at each other"), reflect each child's point of view to let them know they're being heard, describe the problem for them, express faith in their ability to work out a solution, then leave the room and let them handle it. When the situation could get dangerous it's time to acknowledge that things are getting out of hand and to enforce the rules against verbal abuse or physical aggression. If the situation is definitely dangerous, meaning that harm is imminent or has already occurred, adult intervention is necessary and the children should be physically separated for a cooling-off period.

The story of Theo and Donna below shows how sibling rivalry can develop, and then heat up. It also taught their parents a lesson about fairness.

THE STORY OF THEO AND DONNA

Donna was born five years after Theo. Usually this difference in age span lessens the intensity of sibling rivalry, but you couldn't persuade their parents of that! Theo had been an only child and was frankly treated like a prince prior to his sister's birth. He was initially excited about his mother's pregnancy and the prospect of having a brother or sister to play with. When Donna arrived, however, Theo was perplexed to discover that she consumed much of their parents' time and attention. She cried all the time and wasn't much fun to play with. He spent more of his time playing outside with his friends while his mother took care of the baby and her home business. Theo was also a very bright boy, and excelled in school from the beginning. Donna may have gotten attention for being cute, but he was getting plenty of attention for his good grades.

Small Skirmishes, Then War

By the time Donna became a toddler, Theo was set with a circle of buddies, his video game collection, and his schoolwork to keep him busy. To him, his little sister was mostly annoying. She tried to keep up with him around the house, and could not stay out of his room even when she was repeatedly admonished for it. One day, Theo found a sticky lollipop in his video game console and went screaming into the living room where his sister was working on a coloring book. Their shocked mother pointed out that she was only a baby and didn't know any better, and besides Theo was too old to be los-ing his temper toward his sister like that! When a number of his CDs ended up on the bathroom floor, so did Donna. She wailed and cried that Theo pushed her. He admitted to it, and lost his CDs and video games for a week. Things got worse from there.

Donna became very good at competing for their parents' atten-tion when Theo was doing his homework. He became very good at teasing her, even when she had a friend over to play. Often this ended with Donna in tears over how mean her brother treated her. He was impatient with her when they were out in public, and resented having to watch her at home. She was a pest, and he always had other things to do rather than play with her or try to be nice to her. Not only that, but their parents always took her side! This never failed to make him feel upset.

His parents, on the other hand, simply could not understand how this bright and friendly boy could be so polite to everyone but tease his sister endlessly and even get into shoving and push-ing matches with her. How could he be so jealous of his younger sister? Didn't they treat both children equally, and love them equally? They cracked down on him when he became physically aggressive with her and grounded him from going out. He had to learn how to be nicer to her, his mother declared, and that was that. She was smaller than him and could get hurt from their shoving matches.

A Lesson for Mom

One day when Donna was six, she was watching Tom and Jerry car-toons on TV with her mother. Tom the cat was always chasing after poor little Jerry, but of course the mouse usually got the better of him. Donna looked up at her mom with a big grin on her face. "That's like me and Theo," she said proudly. "What do you mean, that's like you and Theo?" her mother asked. "I'm Jerry and he's Tom," the little girl said proudly. "He's bigger than me but I always get him in trouble so I win!" Her mother's jaw dropped as she looked at her little angel beaming on the couch. Then mom had a good laugh.

After that day, when the children played too roughly or got physically aggressive they were both sent to their rooms and punished equally. It did not matter if "he did it" or "she did it," and the cries of "it's not fair" went nowhere. When there were no longer any "winners" in the harassment and blaming game, the teasing and baiting died down considerably. Each child was encouraged to pursue their own interests and was praised for their own accomplishments. Donna became less of a pest, and Theo became less of a meanie. They still teased each other at times but the physical aggression stopped.

Despite our best intentions as parents, it is never possible to treat our children equally. We cannot give them equal time, love, money, or help with their homework. Rather than trying to treat them equally, it's more realistic to try and treat them fairly. It is okay for older children to get a bigger allowance than their younger siblings, or to have a later bedtime. It's okay to spend more time with one child on homework when the child has a project to finish or a test to study for. The parents need to set the values, priorities, and rules for the family. As long as those priorities and rules are enforced fairly, most children will respect them. They may grumble and complain at times that a brother or sister is getting more than their share, but over time we hope things even out.

Child-Rearing Is Not Comparison Shopping: Don't Label or Compare

Children will naturally compete with each other, in their own way, on their own level. Parents can sometimes heighten the sibling rivalry through their own behavior by increasing the level of competition. Sometimes parents will favor one child over another, although they may deny it forcefully when it's brought up to them. The favoritism might have to do with the child's temperament, personality, looks, success in certain areas, or weaknesses. Another way for parents to intensify sibling rivalry is to label their children. If Tom is labeled as "the smart one" among the kids, rest assured that Jason will feel like "the dumb one" and will compete with Tom as well as resent him! Labeling a child almost always causes resentment and jealousy.

Most children will naturally compare themselves with each other, in the process of establishing who they are, and also of establishing their particular role within the family. Unwitting parents can make the sibling rivalry worse by comparing the children in negative ways or even in positive ways. A simple rule of thumb is: Don't compare them!

Rather than comparing a child in a negative way ("Billy always hangs up his coat, why can't you do that too?"), focus instead on the behavior which displeases you or needs to change ("I get upset when I see your coat on the floor in the hallway, please hang it up in the closet"). Rather than comparing the child even in a positive way ("you're a better writer than Billy"), describe only the behavior that pleases you ("your writing is coming along great, I'm really proud of you"). Each child is unique, and it's very important to appreciate the differences. When a parent focuses on each child's unique strengths, without contrasting them to anyone else, it sets a tone more of appreciation than of competition.

It Gets Better

The beleaguered parent may wish to keep in mind that nothing in life lasts forever, not even (in most cases) sibling rivalry. Relationships change and evolve over time as people mature and change. Most siblings learn to get along better, to settle their conflicts, and to accept their differences. The kids who can't stand each other and come to blows over which TV show to watch often end up being the best of friends as they mature into adults. The parents who help them keep sibling rivalry and childhood conflicts from getting out of hand, and teach them some skills for getting along better, with minimal incidents involving blood and broken bones, will have done their jobs well.

Chapter **18**

Respect the Need for Privacy and Individuality

A strong, healthy family is a close-knit *group* made up of *individuals*. Both "group" and "individual" are important defining characteristics in the makeup of the family. While there is a sense of shared responsibility, values, and common heritage, an important job of the family is to raise children who develop into independent adults and can venture out on their own. One seemingly paradoxical role of parents is to raise children who grow up and develop so that they no longer need them! Some parents are so conflicted over the demands of this role, and struggle with it, that they try to keep children in dependent, childlike roles even as the children grow into adulthood. This is not healthy for the parents and can be disastrous for the children.

DON'T SNOOP OR SMOTHER

Individuality, a right to privacy, and independence are qualities to be nurtured within all healthy families. These need to be promoted for all family members, even as the individual members enjoy the comfort and benefits of being part of the family. You are part of us, the message conveys, but you are also free to be yourself and we honor and respect that freedom. Each person within the family is an individual, unique in certain ways, different from everyone else. People also change as they go through different stages in life, and these developmental changes should be respected as well. Every individual needs to be accepted and appreciated for who they are, and allowed to be themselves as they grow and mature.

This is what separates a healthy family from a cult or a gang. For that matter, it also separates a healthy family from an unhealthy one. Cults make every effort to destroy individuality, limit independence and privacy, and make the person conform to group thinking and behavior. They weaken the individual by making the person believe that he or she cannot survive outside the security of the cult structure. Cults make the person feel like a traitor if they question group values or behaviors, and stifle independence of thought or behavior.

Controlling Families   Unhealthy, controlling families tend to take the same approach. Often the parents are over-controlling and insist that children conform so much that a child's freedom to think, act, or even feel becomes severely limited. Acts of individuality may be criticized or punished as signs of "rebelliousness" if they do not meet with the parents' expectations or approval. A healthy family provides security, but also promotes a sense of individuality and independence of thinking that strengthens each family member, and allows them to function and succeed once they leave the family and are on their own. This can be a tricky goal to achieve, but crucial for the health and happiness of the individuals within the family.

The Importance of Privacy

Even the closest couple needs time away from each other at times, and even the closest family needs time for people to be alone. The need for privacy is a fundamental human need. This includes privacy of person, to be oneself and not controlled or manipulated by others. It includes privacy of space, to have a place that is one's own. Even very young children take pride in having "my room," or "my toys," or "my chair" at the dining room table. A healthy family knows to respect everyone's privacy, and not to invade their space. That's what makes living together comfortable, even tolerable. A family that does not respect privacy will find itself struggling with loss of trust, more anger and resentment, less cooperation, and more discipline problems.

A sense of privacy involves the right to be yourself, to "have a life" that is uniquely yours. That means being different in some ways that you choose for yourself—tastes in music, food, clothes, hairstyle, jewelry, choice of jobs, and choice of friends. These differences need to be accepted, even celebrated, as long as they are not harmful or dangerous, and don't infringe on the rights of others.

Green Hair versus Tattoos   The fifteen-year-old who comes home from a friend's house with her hair dyed green is making a statement, all right. But what exactly is that statement? It is probably not "I don't respect my parents wishes" as much as it says "I want to decide who I am, let me find out." Hair grows out, or it can be dyed back, which makes a shouting match or punishment for the behavior seem unnecessary and excessive.

A tattoo may be a different matter, because it involves permanent physical changes. This is where expectations between parents and children need to be clarified and communicated. What is acceptable, at what age? What is not acceptable at a certain age, or not acceptable at *any* age? If parents, children, and teens have discussions about these issues, and that happens in a tone of caring and respect, reaching agreement is not as difficult as many parents might expect. Having a close relationship to begin with makes it much easier to agree, cooperate, and respect each other's wishes.

There are things that are shared between friends, or between siblings, which parents don't have a "right" to know about. The exceptions are matters that pose serious health or legal risks to the child or to someone else. When an intrusive parent is told by a resentful child to "get a life and leave me alone," usually said loudly and with feeling, the real message may be "don't suffocate me and live my life for me." The parent needs to be very honest about the degree to which she or he is over-concerned about the child's behavior, and may indeed be intrusive and over-controlling. If the issue is not clear, an honest talk with a friend or other third party might help to clarify the situation.

The Battle of the Messy Room

In the history of parent-child relationships in contemporary American life, few things have sparked as many conflicts, irritation, and shouting matches as the ongoing battle over the kid's messy room. "Clean your room," the parent says with the usual tone of frustration. "It is clean!" the child responds. "Besides, I cleaned it two days ago!" "You call *that* clean?" the parent retorts, voice rising, pointing out the clothes and toys on the floor and the five empty glasses on the dresser. "You can't find anything in this room, look at that pile of stuff on your desk." "I know where all my stuff is, leave me alone," the child answers defensively, feeling criticized and attacked. "Young man, you clean your room now, put away your toys, and make your bed, or you're not going to the movies tonight," the parent declares, arms folded over chest, firmly putting his foot down. "I hate living in this house, you're so mean!" the child yells in exasperation. Another Saturday afternoon spent fuming and grumbling.

How much aggravation, and how much of an ongoing battle is a clean room worth? If there is an ongoing battle, is it really worth the fight? This is where parents need to make a distinction between what is necessary (no dirty dishes or glasses in the room, it's unsanitary and unhealthy), what is desirable (make your bed every day), and what is frivolous or excessive (pick up and vacuum your room every day). Ask yourself if it's necessary for a child to clean their room more than once a week. But what if the room gets messy two days later, and it aggravates dad or mom to walk through the hallway and see the mess? Simple—close the door. What about teach-

ing the child cleanliness and responsibility? Do we want her growing up to be a slob? Actually there is no evidence whatsoever that
kids with clean rooms grow up to be more responsible, successful,
or cleaner than kids whose rooms are usually messy.

The Child's Space   There is another issue in the messy room battle
besides the parents' cleanliness/responsibility issue. The child's issue
is sometimes a "this is my space, I want to decide what to do with it"
issue. This need for the child to have a space of their own, and have
a sense of privacy within that space, needs to be acknowledged and
respected. There are limits to privacy of course, particularly when
health and safety are involved, but otherwise this need should be
treated seriously. The child's comfort level, in terms of feeling
accepted and feeling safe to be who they are, relies on having their
privacy respected. It is usually not a good idea for a parent to search
a child's room, for example, or go through the child's belongings,
unless there is good cause *and* the child is present during the search.

Chapter **19**

The Perils of Divorce

D ivorce rates have been kept in the United States since 1867, just after the Civil War ended. At that time, the rate was one divorce for every 3,000 people per year. By 1911, it slowly increased to one divorce for every 1,000 people. By 1980, it was up to five divorces for every 1,000 people, or fifteen times as frequent compared to a hundred years earlier (Wolchick & Karoly, 1988). These days about half of all first marriages will end up in divorce, and about 50 to 60 percent of second marriages.

DON'T USE THE KIDS AS EMOTIONAL PAWNS

The average divorce in the United States involves custody of two children under the age of eighteen. The average age of a child involved in a divorce is eight years old. These are very tender years and involve impressionable youngsters who are put in a situation where the parents' divorce changes their lives in profound ways.

Divorce has an emotional impact on children. It can also affect school performance, relationships with peers, and even the child's physical health. It is not simply a matter of the father being absent from the "regular" household, as is sometimes thought. Children react differently to divorce than to the death of a parent, or to being born and raised in a single-parent household. Antisocial behavior and the acting out of problems, for example, are much more common in children whose parents are divorced, as compared to children in families where one of the parents has died (Felner, et al.,

1988). What research has shown, which is surprising to many people, is that what affects children the most is not the divorce as such but rather the "quality" of the divorce and the life conditions which follow the breakup of the marriage.

Divorce Can Be Good or Bad

It is not always true that divorce is bad for children. What may be worse for the kids is being part of a family where the parents are having a horrible marriage, with ongoing conflicts and fights. A "good" divorce where the parents are living apart and making a good effort to get along and parent the children, is usually better than a "bad" marriage where family life becomes an ongoing battle. Of course most children, and parents too, would prefer that the parents have a good marriage and a stable family life. Next in order of preference is a "good" divorce. A bad marriage or a bad divorce can make life seem like a living hell for the adults and children too.

An angry, acrimonious divorce can cause a lot of emotional damage all the way around. Unfortunately, the divorcing or divorced parents, caught up in their battle with each other, not to mention legal and financial problems, may be least accessible for the children just when the kids need them most. This chapter is not so much about how to have a "good" divorce, but about how to minimize the damage for the children and provide responsible and nurturing parenting. Responsible parents don't neglect their children after divorce, and don't use the children as pawns in their battles with the estranged former spouse. The implications of a divorce are that the marriage has failed. It should not mean that the parents are not capable of, or are no longer responsible for, continuing to be loving and effective parents.

Children's Reactions to Divorce   They are shaped to a large degree by the way the parents continue to treat each other, what kind of relationship each child has to each parent, and how stable the new households are. The age and gender of the child can make a difference in her ability to adjust. So can the reactions and attitudes of relatives, neighbors, and influential adults. There is no question that divorcing will have an impact; the real question is what kind and how large it will be. Parents have more control over this than they might assume, depending on how constructive or destructive their own behavior is.

How to Tell the Children About the Coming Divorce

Once a firm decision has been made to get a divorce, and arrangements made for a separation, both parents together should tell the kids about the decision. It is best to tell them all together in a group, not separately or split up in age groups. A good time to make the announcement is about two or three weeks before the parent moves out—not while dad is packing his bags! How much should the children be told about the reasons for the separation or divorce? This is where good judgment must be used. In general, kids should be told what is appropriate for them to know. As Dr. Fitzhugh Dodson writes in *How to Single Parent,* a parent should "tell the truth and nothing but the truth, but you do not need to tell the whole truth." Even very difficult situations can be discussed, if done in a way that is not judgmental and blaming.

It Is Important to Let the Children Know that the Divorce Was Not Their Fault Children very often feel guilty when their parents separate and go through a divorce, but need to be told that they did not cause the divorce. Children do not cause divorces, adults do. This message should be given more than once, during the initial announcement, during the separation, after the divorce, and for as long as necessary. The doubts and guilt the children may feel can stay with them for a long time.

It is not a good idea to lie about who wanted the divorce, or pretend that it's "mutual" if it's not, because the children will soon figure it out anyway from the parents' behavior and attitudes. It is also not a good idea for one or both parents to play the good guy role, while placing the other in the bad guy role. Children want the approval of both parents, and will not be comfortable if asked to choose sides.

Children Should Be Given a Chance to Express Their Feelings Without being censored, judged, or criticized, children need to let out how they feel. It is not realistic or fair to expect that they "should" feel one way or another. People cannot control feelings, only behavior. Children should also be allowed to ask whatever questions they have. Many of these may be very practical questions. Who will I live with? Where will we live? What school will I go to? Will I still see my friends? Will we have enough money to live on? Who gets the dog, cat, or other pets? These questions are important and should be answered respectfully. If a question is too personal or not appropriate to get into with the children, that should be made clear in a calm, noncritical way. Be prepared to answer questions about the divorce for a long time, even long after the divorce is final.

Ten Things Not to Allow to Happen to Your Kids After You Get Divorced

A study at Arizona State University which involved 128 children from divorced families looked at the most stressful divorce related events (Sandler et al., 1988). The ten most toxic, emotionally damaging events are listed and briefly discussed below. Keep in mind that these are not theoretical problems, but rather these are things which the children listed as events that *actually happened to them.*

1. *Don't tell your child that the divorce is his/her fault.* It takes a very sick, or temporarily distraught parent to blame the failure of a marriage on a child, and most parents would never dream of doing such a thing. Some parents are that sick, however, and this still does happen sometimes. The emotional effects on the

child can be devastating. Most children are afraid that some-how the divorce was their fault, and parents usually need to reassure them that they were not responsible for the marriage breaking up.

2. *Don't hit each other or physically hurt each other.* When this hap-pens, particularly in front of the children, the emotional trauma can be severe. Kids simply want their parents to get along with each other and provide a stable family. Physical abuse is the antithesis of this wish, the worst thing for the children to expe-rience. If you find yourself getting angry enough to want to hit, walk away immediately and cool off. It may be necessary to work with a therapist on anger control and conflict resolution.

3. *Don't allow the relatives to criticize the other parent.* Let's face it, divorce brings with it feelings of anger and resentment for the extended family and other relatives, not just the two ex-spouses. Although relatives may have good intentions about defending the parent they feel loyal to, or somehow "setting the child straight" about the other parent, criticizing the other par-ent is always destructive for the child. Tell the relatives and friends to "butt out" when it comes to criticizing or blaming the parents in front of the children.

4. *Don't tell your child that you don't like him/her to spend time with the other parent.* Most children love both their parents, and need to feel loved by both. They don't want to be pulled in two direc-tions, or to have divided loyalties between two divorced parents who don't get along. If you as a parent have a problem with the child spending time with your ex, then bring it up with the judge. Leave the child out of this poisonous dispute.

5. *Don't argue in front of the child.* This is always a good rule, whether the parents are married, separated, or divorced. The child doesn't care "who's fault it is," and ends up being hurt by the expression of aggression between the two people the child loves most. Take your arguments behind closed doors, or even better, to a location where the children are not around to hear you.

6. *Don't say bad things about the other parent in front of the child.* See the point above about divided loyalties. If you need to complain or bitch about your ex, call a friend or see a therapist. Leave the child out of it.

7. *Don't make the child give up pets or other things that he/she likes.* The divorce should not punish the child, nor deprive the child of the things that provide comfort and stability if it can be avoided. Allow the child to keep pets, favorite toys, and valued possessions.

8. *Don't act unhappy in front of the child because of the divorce.* Chances are the child is already experiencing mixed feelings, sadness, confusion, and guilt about the divorce. If you as a parent are hurting over the divorce, which is both common and understandable, talk to a family member, friend, or therapist and get the support and guidance you need.

9. *Don't ask the child questions about the ex-spouse's private life.* No child of divorced parents should be placed in the position of acting as a spy or informant for one or both of the parents. It brings up too many issues of divided loyalty and guilt. If you feel the temptation to ask your child questions about the other parents' social life, friends, finances, and so on, resist the temptation and ask the ex-spouse directly instead. If that is not possible, then live with the ambiguity.

10. *Don't allow people in the neighborhood or community to criticize the other parent to the child.* This is the same principle that was discussed above with regards to the child's relatives, for the same reasons. Well-intentioned neighbors may be tempted to show their loyalty to you by criticizing the ex-spouse. The child is the one who ends up being hurt. Ask the neighbors directly not to criticize the ex-spouse in front of the child, if you see this happening.

What the Children Need

Tell Them They're Not to Blame It is common for children to have some feelings of guilt over their parents' divorce, and sometimes to blame themselves for the divorce if they don't have a better explanation. Young children in particular may believe that the parents divorced because the child is a "bad" child. Some children will try, during the course of a rocky marriage or following the divorce, to be extremely "good" in the hopes that it will prevent divorce or will somehow bring the parents back together. These assumptions involve wishing for a level of control which no child ever has over his parents' marriage.

Tell Them They Will Be Taken Care Of   Divorce is frightening for children because it upsets their world in very basic ways. They need to know that their parents still love them. Basic questions should be provided, such as where the children will live, how visitation will be handled, what school they will attend, and so on. They need to know that their world will not be ending, but rather changing in some ways. Don't assume that children will know these things. Allow them to ask questions, pay attention to their fears and anxieties, and respond to their questions directly and honestly.

Give Them Some Explanation That Is Honest and Makes Sense to Them
Children don't need to know every detail about the parents' reasons for deciding to divorce. Indeed, sharing all the painful problems with the children would not be appropriate nor healthy. Most children want to have some understanding, however, about the reasons for the parents' divorce which provides enough of the truth and makes sense to them. The parents need to be sensitive to the child's maturity level in terms of how much they can understand. Even young children can understand the concept that sometimes people will be happier living apart than living together. They may not like hearing that explanation, of course, but they can understand it and gain a context that explains all the changes in the family's life.

When children don't have an explanation they will likely do what all human beings do when we lack the necessary facts, namely, make some assumption, based on guesswork. One five-year-old girl, whose parents never spoke to her directly about the reasons for their divorce, spent several years living with guilt and shame because she assumed that the reason for the parents' divorce was her refusal to eat her carrots at dinner. She did not want to eat her carrots one night, it led to an argument between the parents, and later that night the parents decided they were getting divorced. The sad thing is that they had no idea this poor girl would make an assumption that placed the blame for their marital problems and divorce on her little five-year-old shoulders. The guilt she suffered for years might have been prevented if at least one of the parents had sat down with her and had a direct and honest conversation about their reasons for divorcing.

Try to Keep Their Lives as Stable as Possible Divorce brings about changes in many areas of a family's life, of course. Drastic changes and loss of stability may cause a great deal of anxiety and feelings of helplessness for the children. All children need a sense of stability and security of course, both physical and emotional. Staying in the same house, attending the same school, keeping the same friends, and attending their usual soccer games and other social activities helps to provide a much needed sense of stability and emotional comfort level. While one or both of the parents may wish to "get a fresh start" and make major changes in their environment, this is rarely what the children hope for, or welcome, or need.

Make Both Parents Accessible and Keep Them Involved One of the common fears for children following divorce is of being emotionally abandoned by the parents. The parents' job is to allay these fears, not simply through verbal reassurance but also through their physical presence and continued involvement in the child's activities. The parents should of course be available by phone when the child wishes to call. One of the most destructive influences in a divorce is the parent who literally does abandon the children emotionally, either because he or she is narcissistic and self-absorbed or because the parent has serious emotional problems or problems with substance abuse. In those situations, the parent is severely lacking and needs to address their own problems more directly via professional help.

What the Parents Can Do

As mentioned above, parents can have a good deal of influence over the "quality" of their divorce. Parents' desire for a decent divorce will have direct consequences on how well the children will be able to cope and adjust.

Resolve Your Differences as Much as Possible and Try to Get Along with Each Other This may be the single biggest factor in how well the family copes with the divorce. There is a great deal of research which shows us that when conflict between the parents is high, emotional stress and tension are high for everyone, and the children have difficulty adjusting and coping with life. Interestingly, this is true not only for divorced families, but also for families that are intact. The amount of parental conflict, both pre- and post-divorce, is a good predictor of dysfunction for the children. This is also associated with poor or inconsistent discipline, and inconsistent or lacking nurturing, which of course cause problems regardless of marital status.

It is imperative then that the parents find a middle ground where they can agree on the major decisions that affect their children's lives and work together on some common goals. While "staying together for the sake of the children" does not apply if the marriage is bad and conflict ridden, on the other hand "getting along for the sake of the children" certainly has a lot to recommend it. "That's easier said than done" is the lament of many angry and resentful parents fresh out of divorce court, however the destructive alternative to getting along should be kept firmly in mind. No one ever said that dealing with divorce was easy, and it's certainly never simple. It remains the parents' shared responsibility to make whatever arrangements are necessary, and seek whatever help they find necessary to deal with their anger and pain and to work with the ex-spouse as well as possible.

Maintain the Children's Stable Lifestyle as Much as Possible   As mentioned above, it is essential for the children's emotional health to have a well-organized, stable, predictable home environment following the divorce. As a rule of thumb, the more changes there are in the children's living conditions, the more difficulty they will have adjusting. These include changes in economic well-being, quality and location of housing, and stability of interests and activities. When the mother-headed household has financial difficulties, adjustment is poorer for the kids because their usual activities are likely to change as well. A stable home environment means similar (but not necessarily identical) expectations, rules, and responsibilities. If one parent is lenient and the other strict, or one a big spender while the other is miserly, it creates confusion for the children and inevitably resentment toward the less permissive or indulgent parent who is being "unfair" in the child's expectations.

Make Custody and Visitation Arrangements a Top Priority and Respect the Agreements Made   While some parents may be tempted to punish the ex-spouse by denying visitation or time spent with the children, this is always a destructive ploy which ends up harming the children more than the ex-spouse. In general, the fewer conflicts in this area the better for everyone. Children must not—ever—be treated as ammunition in the battles between the parents. Custody rights have to be respected, and the visitation schedule made predictable. An important factor that affects children's ability to adapt to divorce is how successfully the parents can establish new and stable relationships with the children. The more contact the child has with both parents, and the more positive the contact, the better the child is able to adjust to all the other changes in her or his life.

In summary, while divorce affects everyone in the family, to a large degree the ways in which it affects family members and how much it affects them is directly related to how the parents deal with the situation. A "good" divorce can be a healthier thing for everyone concerned, adults and children alike, than a "bad" marriage which is characterized by ongoing battles and emotional turmoil. In any divorce, the adults end up divorcing each other, of course, and not their children. A failed marriage does not end the parents' responsibilities to continue caring for and nurturing their children. If divorce happens, the responsible parents will make every effort to keep their anger and resentment in check, agree on basic arrangements for dealing with their children's needs, and continue to be a vital part of their children's lives. If a parent finds it difficult to do that, the responsibility is to seek professional help and support and deal with personal problems related to the divorce so that those problems don't interfere with parental responsibilities.

Chapter **20**

The Challenges of the Single Parent

S ingle-parent families have become a common feature in our society. Usually the single-parent family is headed by a woman; more than 90 percent of single parents are mothers. In some cases, women who are unmarried decide to have children and enter into motherhood by choice. More commonly, a family breaks up due to divorce or the death of a spouse. The result of divorce and death is that a great many number of children experience the stress and trauma of a broken family.

DON'T BE INTIMIDATED BY THE CHANGES AND RESPONSIBILITIES OF SINGLE PARENTHOOD

Single-parent families tend to have more stressors. In the case of a divorce, the parents may end up having ongoing conflicts long after the divorce decree becomes official. If a single parent is also a working mother, the stress level rises even more. The single parent is likely to find life becoming much more stressful due to having sole responsibility for financial and household matters. The former partner is no longer there to bounce ideas off, share the workload, share household expenses and financial worries, help with disciplining the children, and look after the kids during particularly hectic times or business trips.

Single Parenthood Is Not All Bad

A resourceful single parent who provides discipline and love can be a very good parent indeed, superior to many parents who are part of a couple. It is a myth that children growing up in single-parent families have more emotional problems or less success than do children growing up with two parents. The exception may be when the single-parent family is the result of a very bad divorce where the parents continue to battle each other—the children are more likely to have problems whether the parents stay together or end up divorced. As the literature on divorce teaches us, a "good" divorce is often much healthier for everyone involved than a "bad" marriage that is abusive or conflict ridden. Oftentimes there is a re-bonding in the single parent family, and kids become more helpful and cooperative with the primary custodial parent. Children tend to be more responsible, for example with doing chores, helping with meal preparation, and taking care of their own responsibilities such as doing schoolwork.

Single parents can meet new people, choose their friends, and enjoy a renewed social life. This takes time and extra effort of course, but they can choose to participate in happier relationships. Finally, single parents often end up marrying or remarrying. This chapter will deal with the challenges of becoming a single parent, coping with the responsibilities of single parenthood, and the transition into a new married relationship.

Adjusting to Divorce

A divorce causes emotional turmoil for everyone in the family, children and adults alike. The children will likely react by feeling angry, resentful, hurt, and scared. The security they have known in having the parents around has been shattered. Basic questions need to be answered, such as who will I live with, will we have to move, what school will I be going to? Adjusting to divorce and preparing for single parenthood starts with telling the children about the upcoming separation and divorce. Chapter 19 in this book, entitled *The Perils of Divorce,* discusses in more detail how to announce the marital breakup to the children. They need to know that the parents will be honest with them, and will continue to love them and take care of them. Questions will need to be answered, and plenty of reassurance provided.

Whatever the temptations may be during a time of hurt, anger, and conflict, as divorce situations tend to be, it is crucial for everyone's sake to try and get along as well as possible with the divorced spouse. Let go of the past, don't rehash old grievances, and try by all means possible to avoid getting into a hostility cycle with each other. Strive to reach constructive decisions that can benefit everyone. Getting into a blaming contest and trying to win arguments is a losing proposition for everyone. Don't criticize the other parent in front of your children, because that only wounds them deeper.

Playing Fair   Do not, under any circumstances, pressure or force the child to take sides. Children who are pulled in different directions and have their loyalty to one parent challenged may rebel by withdrawing from *both* of you. The kids don't care who's wrong or right, or whose fault it is. They simply want both of you to care about them. When a child does take sides with one parent, as sometimes happens in a sad attempt to make sure that at least *one* parent continues to care, it creates deeper and more serious problems for the child and is a very unhealthy situation.

Custody and Visitation   This must be worked out fairly, and followed by both sides. Joint custody usually works best for children, unless the parents are truly emotionally unhealthy and hostile toward each other. In that situation, the children may feel like they're living in two separate battle zones. Visitation should never become an area of conflict and battle, although unfortunately it often does. Keep in mind that the child needs both of you, and always will.

Even if the absent parent was not an exemplary parent, the child will still miss him or her and look forward to visitation time. Most children will resent deeply the failure of a parent who does not show up for visitation or spend time with them. The emotional loss of living through a divorce is compounded by the emotional hurt of being forgotten or neglected during the parents' visitation time. Think of it, with little exaggeration, as rubbing salt into your child's emotional wounds.

Some parents will play games with visitation rights and try to deny the other parent opportunities to spend time with the children. This immature, vindictive, irresponsible way of trying to punish the ex-spouse ends up hurting the children much more. Unless there is actual abuse going on, as determined by a health professional and supported by a court, no parent should be denied access to a child. Some parents, most commonly fathers who may have only visitation rights, will simply drop out of their children's lives or see them very infrequently or sporadically. The sense of abandonment on the children's part can be profound when that happens, with emotional damage that can last a lifetime. Is any amount of marital conflict or anger toward your ex-spouse worth abandoning your children?

Adjusting to Widowhood

Dealing with the death of a loved one is one of the most painful events in life. When a parent becomes terminally ill, or dies suddenly in an accident, the shock and burden on the surviving parent and children can be enormous. This is where seeking and receiving support becomes a necessity, not a luxury. Everyone is going to be in emotional shock for a period of time, then going through a process of mourning. If the dying parent has a long terminal illness, the children should be told about the expected outcome if they ask. Otherwise it may be best to wait until a month or so before the expected death. Young children may not have a good understanding of what death is, but if they ask they should be told the truth in a way that makes sense for them. If the death is sudden and unexpected, the children should be told immediately, and together as a group if possible.

Following the death of the spouse, the surviving parent needs to take care of herself or himself. This means going through mourning and doing the grief work. A therapist who works with grief and bereavement issues might be a big help during this period. Joining an emotional support group, offered by a hospital, hospice, church, or synagogue, may also be very helpful. A bereavement support group allows and encourages sharing the feelings, fears, and solutions to problems that a newly widowed individual must deal with. Such a group can be a powerful, healing experience.

The mourning process should be explained to the children. They need encouragement to share whatever feelings they have, and be provided with love and support when sad and unhappy feelings come up. It is better to mourn early, and let feelings out, rather than to shy away from painful feelings and delay the mourning process. No family member should be pushed into hurrying up the grieving process of course, but simply encouraged to share feelings and given support when they do. Mourning takes longer than most people think, and certainly longer than we allow in our culture. Grieving the loss of a loved one for six months to a year, or longer, is perfectly normal and should be expected.

Helping Children Adjust

Whether due to divorce or widowhood, every family that becomes a single-parent family is likely to go through phases of adjustment. The lives of the adults and children are disrupted in major, often traumatic ways. Children may respond in their own idiosyncratic ways, depending on the age of the child, personality, and relationship with the parents. Even infants and babies will feel the emotional changes in a family brought on by divorce or widowhood. An infant is very capable of sensing the loss of emotional nurturance from the absent parent, increased feelings of sadness or anger, and increased emotional stress. The custodial parent, at times overwhelmed by new responsibilities and going through a rough time emotionally, may also not be as available physically or emotionally to the young child as he or she was prior to the separation, divorce, or death.

A toddler just learning basic skills such as walking, and developing vocabulary and speech, will miss the presence of the absent parent, and may also find that the caretaker parent is less involved and attentive. Preschool children are much more capable of expressing feelings verbally, and should be encouraged to discuss their feelings, concerns, and needs. Allow them to verbally express whatever is going on within, even if the feelings are negative or critical of the parents. Young children experiencing the loss of a parent may show an intense, increased need for love and affection. Children of all ages need hugs and other forms of affectionate touch to provide reassurance and nurturing, but particularly after the loss of a significant other.

Natural Hostility Preteens and young teenagers just developing their own sense of identity and independence may react with increased rebelliousness, as they try to deal with their own anger and fears. Boys in particular, in a family undergoing divorce, may become angry at their mother and blame her for the father's absence. Adolescents may react to divorce with a great deal of anger toward both parents, and become even more involved in the peer group than usual. Whereas younger children may demand more affection, the adolescent is likely to express hostility and a greater need for distance. As difficult as it may be to believe at the time, the teen may be intensely angry at the situation of divorce and breakup of the family, and does not truly hate the parents. He will eventually get over the hostile and angry attitude.

Children of all ages will likely develop deep feelings of sadness that color their outlook on the world, people, and life. In the case of divorce, the child's sadness may be covered up by increased feelings of anger, rebelliousness, and temper tantrums. When this happens they will likely need more comforting, as well as discipline if the behavior gets out of hand. Following the death of a parent, the reaction will likely be one of deep sadness. The children may worry about losing the remaining parent, and about who will take care of them. Feelings of being rejected by the absent parent are very common among children, whether the loss is due to divorce or even to the death of a parent.

Helping Children Adjust to the Loss of a Parent   This requires understanding, caring, and patience. This is not easy to do for a parent who is also going through a very stressful period of adjustment. Support and help is necessary from family, friends, or a helping professional in cases where the person is having a particularly difficult time adjusting to the changes in the family. Children may act out their anger behaviorally in destructive ways, have their school performance deteriorate, or become withdrawn and depressed. For that matter, parents might experience difficulties coping emotionally and find themselves struggling at work or at home, withdrawing from others, or trying to escape through increased drinking or using other substances. When faced with that situation, the parent must do the responsible thing and get appropriate help for themselves. An adult who is not taking good care of himself or herself will not be able to take good care of their children either.

Survival Skills for the Single Parent

The adult who faces single parenthood must become a terrific juggler of time, people, and obligations. The custodial parent becomes largely responsible for health care, school problems, transportation to activities, helping make plans, listening to complaints, setting and enforcing rules, providing discipline, paying bills, shopping, cooking, laundry, and bedtime stories. And, by the way, don't forget to have a life of your own and take time for friends and social activities! The time pressures and responsibilities can easily seem overwhelming. At the same time it is not healthy for you as a parent to live your life for your children. You *must* take care of yourself too, and have a life as an adult apart from your family life.

Seeking and Accepting Support from Family and Friends This is one essential first step. Make friends with other parents, and trade off babysitting chores once in awhile. Grandparents can make wonderful, often appreciative babysitters who enjoy their time with the grandchildren. Many grandparents are happy to provide some day care functions after school until the parent gets home from work. This is not necessarily an imposition, but part of childrearing practices as old as the human race. The grandparents need to be asked of course, and agree to it, and not watch the children because of pressure or guilt. Even if they don't ask for or accept any money for the day care responsibilities, it is a nice gesture to buy them a gift of appreciation once in awhile. Grandparents can be valuable teachers for the children, as well as providing emotional nurturance. And if they spoil the grandkids a little, so what? One of the simple joys of childhood is being spoiled by one's grandparents.

The single parent must take time to make adult friends, and maintain those friendships. Having one or two close friends can be a lifesaver when you need to blow off some steam, vent frustration, get some quick advice, or simply have some adult conversation. You need some friends just for the sake of friendship, where there is no romantic involvement. In time you will probably want to start dating again. The kids won't mind, and in fact may even encourage you to do it. It can be very uncomfortable for children to see a parent feeling lonely and unhappy. Children provide some companionship of course, but they are not a substitute for adult relationships. Most children don't want a parent depending on them for companionship, as it often generates feelings of pressure and guilt, inability and anger. Parents want their children to develop relationships with peers and "play with someone your own age," and they should apply the same principle to themselves.

Everyone Needs a Good Stress-management Strategy Considering the amounts of pressure and stress single parents go through, this becomes even more important. Do you have a "safe" outlet for anger and frustration? Find a close friend, family member, or therapist who can serve that function. Vent when necessary, but never to the child! Find time to exercise, even if only a brisk walk after dinner, in the morning, or during your lunch break. Few things are as effective in managing stress as regular, aerobic exercise. Get enough sleep, or as much as possible. Late-night movies on TV are not as good for you as you might think if you're tired and stressed the next day. Eat nutritious foods, as you encourage your children to do. This particular type of role modeling will not only help them, but provide tangible benefits in the way you feel, your energy level, and your ability to cope with stress.

Find something that helps you relax and feel good: a hobby, meditation, praying, writing poetry, painting landscapes, and so on. Give yourself a chance to experience some moments of inner peace, which can help counterbalance the external chaos. Do some things that are fun and relaxing with your children, but also with adult friends when you can spend some time away from the children. This will give you and them an opportunity to break the same old routines and do something different. Be active in your place of worship, or join a service club such as the Rotary Foundation. These often meet around lunchtime, when the children are in school, and won't interfere with family time. Make some time in your schedule which is reserved just for you, and do something spontaneous that will make you feel good—without pressure or guilt! Take an evening class in a subject you enjoy, where you are more likely to meet single adults like yourself with similar interests. All of these activities require planning and effort, but are necessary for a healthy lifestyle for any adult. Don't let pressure, stress, or guilt stop you from pursuing them.

Chapter **21**

Blending, Bonding, Stepparenting

A look at rising divorce statistics, the number of children born to single parents, and the increase in one-parent families are persuading some people that the two-parent family is on the verge of extinction. Nothing could be further from the truth. The two-parent family still does the best job of fulfilling the emotional, financial, and everyday practical needs of both children and adults. In addition to the economic benefits, there can be the sharing of all responsibilities between the two spouses. The "death of the family" myth is exactly that—a myth.

DON'T IGNORE THE CHALLENGES
OF THE STEPPARENT ROLE

Even when people divorce, they often remarry. What has become common in our culture is not the death of the family, but the prevalence of stepfamilies. Forty percent of children born in the United States will experience parental divorce before they reach the age of eighteen. Twenty-five percent of all children in this country will be part of a stepfamily before they reach adulthood. About one-half of all divorced parents remarry within three years of their divorce. Half or more of remarriages end up in divorce within ten years, and thus many of the children involved in divorce will end up in more than one stepfamily arrangement. Stepparenting is here to stay.

Adjustments, Hopes, and Challenges

The challenges for the stepfamily are many. First is to overcome the pain and loss from the breakup of the previous marriage and the old home. It can take a long time to grieve the loss of the old family, and this process is not necessarily over because one or both parents remarry. The parents need to make sure they are "emotionally" divorced from the former spouse, as well as legally and physically divorced. Few things are as destructive for a family, and particularly for the children, than divorced couples who carry on their battles even after the divorce. The children need to maintain relationships with both parents, and be encouraged to do so.

The Fear of the New Marriage Not Working Out   This creates pressure and stress for everyone. It's important for the parents to realize that the children also experience these fears and apprehensions, although they may not be verbalized or discussed. The newly married parents need to clearly define what the rules and expectations are for the new family, and what the appropriate roles are for the adults and children. When possible, the parents need to make sure they reach agreement on basic issues such as discipline, freedoms, and responsibilities. Will the new family accomplish all these tasks? The answer will go a long way toward determining how well the family can blend together, work out their differences and problems, and succeed in building a loving home.

When the stepparents don't have a good understanding from the beginning of what the expectations, goals, and rules of the new family are, conflicts will surely develop and the positive hopes quickly turn to dust. Unrealistic or unspoken expectations are a minefield that will eventually blow up. As comforting as the thought may be of finding instant love and acceptance in a "new" family, unlike the "old" failed one, that wish is usually hoping for too much too soon. Building a new family takes time and will require patience on everyone's part. Developing trust, rules, shared expectations, and stability all take time. Affection cannot be forced or demanded, nor trust, nor closeness. There is no instant recipe for love.

Getting "On the Same Page"

The first crucial step to building trust is acceptance. People will agree at times, disagree at times, find ways to give and take and compromise, but it's vitally important to find a common ground on which all can live. The two families bring with them different expectations, likes and dislikes, habits, and traditions. It's not a matter of one being better than the other, or a matter of right or wrong. One family may be used to making a big deal over Halloween, another over Thanksgiving. Which occasion is more "important" or worthy of celebration may be a matter of opinion. Finding ways to accept, accommodate, and appreciate the differences builds a sense of community and shared values. The feeling of "us" does not come from winning a competition, but rather from cooperating on a common task.

It is the parents' job to define expectations and rules for the new family. This task should begin even during the period of being engaged to each other, long before the marriage ceremony. Where will the family live? How will money be shared? What are reasonable freedoms and responsibilities for the children? How will discipline be handled? Which parent disciplines which children? Will the parents have any more children? How will disagreements be worked out? How will the parents deal with conflicts with the former spouses? All these issues need to be discussed openly, honestly, and directly.

Defining the Stepparent Roles

One of the tasks for the parents is to decide what role each stepparent will play in the lives of the children. Often the stepchild will help define that role, of course, but the adult will strongly influence the nature of the relationship from very early on. Some parents take the extreme approach of either trying too hard to force a close relationship before the children are ready for it, or holding back too much and seeming distant and uninterested. Neither of these attitudes on the part of the stepparent is likely to work out well.

In their book *Strengthening Your Stepfamily,* Elizabeth Einstein and Linda Albert help define several roles which stepparents may fall into. When the stepparent takes the role of being a *friend* to the spouse's children, his or her role is to provide additional support and caring to the stepchildren. The children already have two parents, and rarely wish to have a third. The stepparent in the friend role is usually less threatening to the child, who may understandably have fears that this new adult in his or her life will try to take over and control things, or will try to displace the absent biological parent. Becoming friends over time allows for trust and respect to build. Being a friend to a child is not the same thing as treating the child as an equal or a buddy, of course. The stepparent is still an adult caretaker whose authority needs to be respected. Nevertheless, the friend role for the stepparent has many benefits to recommend it.

When the stepparent Acts as Confidante This role is to become a sounding board or advisor to the stepchild. This can be particularly useful when the stepchild is a teenager. Stepparents to very young children may find themselves in the role of being *another parent figure.* This is particularly true if the child does not have regular contact with one of the biological parents. Even in that case, the stepparent must keep in mind that she is a parent in addition to the biological parent, and not a replacement for the biological parent. It is not healthy for the child or stepparent to discourage affection or loyalty to the absent biological parent. A stepparent who takes the role of *mentor* takes a supportive and teaching role, becoming a special person in the child's life who shares wisdom, knowledge, and advice. Any adult may become a mentor to a young person, helping to guide and prepare them for adult life, and stepparents who develop a close relationship with older stepchildren often assume this role. The stepparent who takes the role of *role model* teaches by setting an example. Children copy the behaviors of parents and other adults, and the stepparent is in a position to play an important part in this type of social learning. Of course, the role model may set a positive example or a negative one, and the stepparent needs to be aware of what type of example he is demonstrating for the children.

The Importance of Consistent Discipline

One of the major problems that newly remarried parents can run into is disagreement about how discipline should be handled. If both parents come into the marriage with children of their own, each has a history of a discipline approach with their own children. One parent may be very strict and no-nonsense, with clear-cut rules that are consistently enforced. Another parent may be much more lax and tolerant, using discussion and compromise in responding to the children's behavior. Either approach may work for that particular parent or particular child. When the family is blended, however, the clash of styles will create confusion and conflict unless the parents can develop some consistency in their disciplinary styles.

When Stepparents and Children Are Thrown Together The children often don't yet have a close enough bond with the stepparent to create an instant family, and thus may not respect the adult's authority. It is common for children in a new marriage to test the stepparent and reject discipline. When that happens, the parents need to make clear what the roles of the parents and children are, and to back up each other when it comes to enforcing discipline.

In the beginning of the new marriage, before a close bond has been established between child and stepparent, many parents find it useful to discipline only their own children. When one parent is out of the house, the parent who is present has authority to discipline all the children. Over time, however, the parents need to develop some shared expectations and consistent approach to discipline. When the children understand that the parents have a relationship based on cooperation and understanding, they are likely to have more respect for the rules and to accept discipline from each parent.

When Things Work Out

Stepparenting carries with it challenges, but also rewards. It can be tremendously gratifying for the new family to build on hopes, overcome fears, build trust, resolve differences, learn acceptance, and develop loving relationships. Creating a healthy family atmosphere starts with the parents, who set the tone and define the goals for all the family members. The parents have to communicate with each other first of all, and then with the children—directly, honestly, and often. Trust requires honesty and intimacy. Feelings need to be brought out into the open, positive as well as negative, or painful, ones. Problems need to be discussed openly and directly. Keeping quiet about problems usually makes them worse, with the risk that they'll spin out of control. Although the parents set the tone, the responsibility for making a stepfamily work is shared by all of its members. The joys of making it work will also be shared by all.

Chapter **22**

Our Fears, Their Needs

T he years between the ages of thirteen and eighteen are often the most volatile and stressful for both parents and children. It is a time of contradictions and conflicts for both teens and parents. The adolescent goes through a period of rapid physical and psychological change. Family relationships get stretched to the breaking point—and sometimes beyond. Knowing how to deal with the process of your child's maturity and search for independence and identity is a key to managing the troublesome teen years.

DON'T MISTAKE TEENAGE
INDEPENDENCE FOR REBELLION

For the teenager, adolescence is a time of tremendous hope and growth. It is also a time of great confusion and insecurity, of searching for a sense of identity. The "who am I" types of questions play a large role in the way adolescents think, feel, and behave. For the parents this is a trying time as well. We want them to grow up, but also fear losing them. There are times when the parent must still exert her authority, and times when it's better to pull back and let things go. This is a tricky push-pull process which changes with time and circumstance, and there are no clear-cut rules. There is no cookbook or recipe for how much freedom to allow a teenager, when to take a firm stand, and when to ease up and let your teen make choices on his own. Most often these decisions depend on the teenager, his level of maturity, and outside circumstances which can also play a part. The challenge for the parent is to know when to let go, and how.

Changes, Changes Everywhere

Expectations change on both sides as children grow into the teen years. Many of the old rules no longer apply. The old ways of discipline no longer work as well. Through the parents' eyes, the playful and loving young child can seem transformed into a rebellious, selfish, ungrateful teenager. "Why don't you grow up!" the parent complains. Through the teenager's eyes, the parents can seem transformed into too-strict worrywarts who try to control everything he does. "You don't understand me!" the teenager cries. In reality both have a point. These seemingly contradictory perceptions are exaggerated, of course, but often these perceptions are the only reality each parent and teen can see. It is also true that everyone, every single one of us, will act on the basis of our perceptions, our unique perceived reality. If we see each other as "the enemy" who neither understands nor cares about us, conflicts and battles will surely follow. Everybody loses in that scenario.

Teens Are from Camelot, Parents Are from the School of Hard Knocks

In his excellent book *Surviving Your Adolescents,* psychologist Thomas Phelan Ph.D. points out correctly that parents and teens don't just *seem* different from each other, in some very basic ways they *are* different. First, teens are full of dreams, and their perception of life is very much shaped by those dreams. The future holds the exciting but bewildering challenges of college, careers, cars, places to go and things to do. Parents on the other hand are focused on the here and now, handling immediate problems, dealing with the mundane realities of life. There are bills to pay, jobs to tend to, and household tasks which never end. For the parents, very often mid-life crisis hits around this time as well, and their dreams are associated not so much with hope anymore but rather with some degree of disillusionment over dreams which never came true. The teen looks at dreams and finds optimism and inspiration. The parent may be much more world weary and cynical. Neither is right, and neither is wrong. The parent and teen are simply looking at life through opposite ends of the telescope.

Breaking Away While Holding On

Second, whereas the major task for teens during this stage of development is to develop independence and break away from the parents, the major task for parents is to learn how to let go in a healthy way of the children they have nurtured since birth. This process results in a continuous tug of war because rarely, if ever, will the teen and the parents be in complete synchrony.

As a matter of pride and psychological health, the teen needs to feel that he or she is growing up and becoming a unique individual. They will sometimes assert this emerging sense of independence in ways that baffle and exasperate the poor beleaguered parents who see their children testing the rules and challenging the parents' authority. Some choices the teens can make are relatively harmless ones, for example in the clothes they wear and their choice of music. Some choices are potentially harmful and even dangerous, such as disobeying curfew, using alcohol and other drugs, and using a car irresponsibly. The wise parent knows—or learns—how to pick her battles carefully. If not, then *everything* becomes a battle.

Why Her Best Friend Tina Knows More Than You

Third, while parents are still invested primarily in their child and place their focus there, teenagers are invested primarily in their friends and peer group and place their main focus there. The teenager who is "almost never home anymore" is acting normally in our culture. He or she is not rejecting the family, but rather searching for a sense of identity and independence away from the family.

The Peer Group   Fellow dreamers and optimists become the reference point for shaping much of their own thinking and behavior. There are shared values among the peer group in clothes, music, speech, hair styles, etc., which differentiate every generation of teens from their parents' generation. The parents are excluded from this process by age and generation, and it is the foolish parent indeed who tries to imitate the teenagers in their dress or behavior. The wise parent will recognize this process, acknowledge it, perhaps even joke about it, but not take it as personal rejection. The teenager's focus on time, interests, and values shared by friends should never lead to accusations of ingratitude, betrayal, or to heaping guilt on the adolescent.

The parent who does not learn to let go and allow the adolescent room to grow will be creating a situation of conflict and never-ending battles. The following story about Brian and his parents illustrates how easily conflicts can emerge, and persist, when parents and teens become warring factions.

BRIAN AND HIS PARENTS

Brian was sixteen years old and a veteran of ongoing fights with his parents over seemingly everything they wanted from him. He was never home except to eat and sleep. He never talked to his parents anymore unless it was to ask for something he wanted. They did not approve of his choice of friends, but of course Brian defended them aggressively against any criticism. He preferred torn blue jeans and baggy shirts, and wore a stud in one ear. He stayed out past curfew at least once per week, then argued over being grounded. Brian was now skipping school, something he had never done before, which concerned his parents greatly. They suspected he drank beer occasionally with his friends, although he of course denied it. His parents were aware of the dangers of drinking and drug use, which they made very clear to Brian. What kind of example was he setting for his younger brother and sister? They caught him lying a few times, which understandably disturbed them. How could they trust him now? Didn't he realize what he was doing to them? Didn't he care?

Brian held a burning anger because, eight months past his sixteenth birthday, he did not yet have his driver's license. His parents considered his behavior too immature and irresponsible for him to handle driving a car. In addition, they wanted him to earn enough money to pay for his car insurance and gas when he started to drive. He was immature and ungrateful. They were hopelessly unfair and controlling. The family was at war.

When Frustration Boils Over

"He's out of control," said Brian's father in a frustrated and angry voice. His face darkened and turned red with anger as he described the latest incident that showed how irresponsible and disrespectful their son had become. Brian had held a summer job at a bowling alley refreshment stand for three weeks, and was doing a good job by all accounts. He then decided to try a new haircut which left his hair longer on the right side than the left. Even more striking, he dyed his hair a forest green color.

Brian never consulted his parents about changing his hair style or color, of course. His friends thought it looked pretty cool, and some of them tried similar experiments. Green, orange, and purple were the preferred colors. His younger siblings giggled and laughed when they first saw it. They soon learned it wasn't funny when their dad started yelling.

To say the least, Brian's parents were not pleased with the changes in their son's appearance. It would also have been nice if they had been asked about it first. They were, after all, still his parents and he was living under their roof. A long and loud argument followed about respect and communication, not to mention good taste.

"It's my hair, not yours!" Brian yelled. "I'll do what I want with it!"

There was no disputing that it was indeed his hair, but the question of his freedom to "mangle" it was hotly contested by his father. Brian's mother tried to make some peace, but she felt a duty to support her husband and was not thrilled about the radical change in her son's appearance either. Brian's father was even more disturbed when Brian was fired from his job. The bowling alley operator did not consider Brian's appearance acceptable for a young man dealing with his customers, and told Brian he was being let go. Family argument No. 2 about the hair was even longer, hotter, and more personal.

"How do you expect anyone to hire you when you look like that?" his father yelled. "Didn't you think ahead before you made yourself look like a circus clown?"

"All you care about is money!" Brian shot back.

The Real Issues

A discussion with Brian and his parents showed that money was not the issue at all. Neither, for that matter, was Brian's disregard for his future or even for his parents. He resented being treated like the "bad guy" in the family. Why didn't his parents trust him with anything? All his friends had their driver's licenses already. He did not commit any crimes, was never arrested, did not do drugs, and was passing all his classes. Why did they treat him like some kind of criminal? "Your goal in life is to control me!" he accused them. Well, he would show them all right who was going to be controlled.

The parents knew that Brian's accusation wasn't true, of course. They were concerned about his safety and his future, and only wanted him to be responsible. The part that was not being communicated directly was the emotional hurt they felt due to Brian's withdrawal from the rest of the family. He'd been distant and angry with them for more than two years now. Were they such bad parents that he had to spite them at every turn? They were only trying to do what was best for him, and for the entire family.

Finding the Common Ground

The real battle between Brian and his parents was not about responsibility, respect, or green hair. As they began to look at the issues from the other's point of view, it became clear that the main issues were independence, freedom, and trust. Brian's parents were not allowing him much room to assert his independence. Even worse, they took his rebelliousness personally as a sign of rejection and lack of caring on his part, which only added hurt to the anger and worry. The power struggles became overdone, and the parents overreacted at times. There was nothing in Brian's history to suggest that he was any less capable than his peers of having a driver's license and the responsibilities of driving.

For his part, Brian pushed against the constraints set by his parents a little too hard. He began to assert his independence by doing things which were harmful, for example breaking curfew and skipping school. It was not possible to ask his parents for trust and increased freedoms when he committed such major infractions. The family battles decreased tremendously when Brian and his parents stopped blaming each other and began to cooperate about each other's major needs. Brian was required to make curfew every day, not miss any school, and not drink alcohol. In return he was allowed to get his driver's license and to use the car two days per week. He was happy to get a part-time job where the employer did not care about the color of his hair, and to contribute to paying for the car insurance. His hair, clothes, and music stopped being an issue. His room had to be picked up once per week but otherwise became a nonissue as well. As more conflicts became resolved and tensions dropped, Brian started spending a little more time at home and playing with his brother and sister. He still spent much of his time with his friends, but he acted more like a part of the family as well and participated in family outings. It was good to have him back, and he was glad to be an *accepted* member of the family.

Teenagers Need Independence the Way Fish Need Water They will find ways to express that need, in one way or another. The parent who does not recognize this and fights the process of seeing the son or daughter pull away will end up in ongoing battles that are unnecessary, destructive, and make the period of adolescence even more stressful than it already is. Needs change, rules change, and behavior requires adjustments and change on the part of the parent as well as the adolescent. Allow breathing room for growth and healthy self-expression. You can still be in control even though you don't rule with an iron glove. Allow your son or daughter safe areas where they can rebel and be themselves, and where any damage will be negligible or very small. Is it really important how clean their room is? Is it worth fighting about for the next four or five years? And how would you feel if someone told you how you had to style your hair? Pick your battles carefully, mom and dad.

The Mutual Need

Don't be shocked to learn that your rebelling adolescent actually wants to get along with you. Teenagers need to show their independence, but they also need your love, acceptance, and discipline when discipline is required. It can be difficult to determine how much freedom and responsibility your teenager can handle, and it will require some trial and error and learning on all sides. The key is to maintain some flexibility, be prepared to negotiate some points which are not worth battling over, and admit when you are wrong. The idealism of youth demands and respects fairness, not capitulation and surrender on the part of parents and other authority figures. Flexibility, fairness, and consideration for the needs of others provide a good lesson in maturity and responsibility, for teens and adults alike.

The Parent Who Remains the Hard-nosed Dictator   When the child reaches adolescence, the parent that provided firm rules and discipline to the younger child and had the child's obedience and respect, will likely find that no longer works. It can be disconcerting to any loving, caring parent to one day find their parenting skills compared with the methods of former Nazi leaders. Who, me? asks the bewildered parent. When did I become the bad guy? The answer is, you're not. And the green-haired youngster you used to play Legos with isn't the bad guy either. If you can anticipate, acknowledge, and accept the changes in your child's behavior that come with adolescence, you can perhaps prevent any major warfare from breaking out. If all of you make it through adolescence with the family intact and no lasting destructive grudges, you will have managed uprisings so as to prevent all-out war.

Chapter **23**

Freedom, Responsibility, and Entitlement: Finding the Balance

"You say you want more freedom,
And that's OK with me,
If you show you can handle,
Responsibility."
— RAP SONG WRITTEN BY DAD FOR TWELVE-YEAR-OLD DAUGHTER

How much freedom can children handle? What kinds of responsibilities should be expected of them? The answers depend a great deal on the child's age and developmental level, and also on the individual child. Some children are simply more mature than others, at any level of development. Other children require more supervision and attention. They will let you know that quite clearly through their behavior. Even within a family, children may differ widely in how much freedom and responsibility they can be trusted with. Wise parents will take their cues from the youngster's behavior, and make decisions and adjustments accordingly.

DON'T GIVE MORE FREEDOMS AND RESPONSIBILITIES THAN CHILDREN CAN HANDLE

Children are very much individuals. They are born with intellectual abilities and an emotional temperament that are "hard-wired" into the brain. Most parents can tell from an early age if a child will be an "easy" child who is mostly pleasant, helpful, and cooperative, or a "difficult" child who will be fussy, temperamental, and challenging to the parent. The "nature versus nurture," or biology versus learning, argument about personality and behavior can only be answered by saying "both." Start with the unique child you get and then work with behavior as you go along, making adjustments for developmental stages and specific events that happen in the child's and the family's life.

Developmental Stages and Expectations

A toddler, from the time she or he starts walking to about the age of two, needs freedom to move around and explore the world. This is when "child-proofing" the house becomes imperative, because there is little that the energetic and curious youngster will not try to get into. The major responsibility expected of the toddler is to obey rules regarding restrictions on his freedoms, and to understand the significance of "no." A toddler does not open the refrigerator door, touch things on the stove, draw with crayons on the wall, or climb on the window ledge for example. The rules for a toddler need to be minimal and then enforced as consistently as possible. The idea is to keep the child out of harm's way, let him play freely, and prevent any serious damage to the premises. Choosing one room or other area of the house where there are things to play with, and simply letting the toddler play there without interference or a hundred no-nos, tends to work to the benefit of both parent and child.

During the "terrible twos" stage, a child starts developing a stronger sense of being independent, and showing it more aggressively. One way to assert independence is to resist whatever the parents want. It's as if the child is saying, "hey look at me, I am thinking for myself!" The responsibility of the child here is to control aggression so that it does not become physical or destructive, to learn basic self-help skills such as brushing teeth and getting dressed, and to learn to accept parental authority in the end.

Between the ages of three and six, the child needs to learn to control impulses better and think through behavior before making a decision or acting on it. Whereas the toddler needs a "no" from the parent to prevent irresponsible behavior, the five-year-old needs to hear "no" from himself. The child also learns how to become less emotionally dependent on the parent, and play more cooperatively with siblings and peers. Communication changes over from physical behavior to verbal for the most part.

The Responsible Kid   The school-age child learns the responsibilities associated with following rules and getting work done. Things are no longer automatically given the child, but must be earned. Assignments need to be organized, spelling words memorized, art projects completed, and accountability to teachers and parents becomes an issue. The child becomes part of a peer group, strongly influenced by friends as well as parents. Between the ages of eleven and thirteen, children start to rebel against society's value system. They no longer see the parents as the omniscient, all-powerful figures young children see. They may in fact become quite obnoxious in their attitude toward the parents. Keep in mind this is part of the process of putting away their childhood identity and replacing it with something that is far from fully formed or consistent. Children at this age are given more responsibilities for chores, and expected to become increasingly independent about school work.

The Rebellious Teen   The rebellious attitude typically intensifies in the teen years. Expect a good deal of unpredictable behavior that is fueled by hormonal changes and personalities in transition. Physical changes leads to increased social awareness, and preoccupation with one's body. Crises may develop over perceptions that the teen is too short, too tall, too fat, too skinny, and so on. Rebelliousness against the parents' wishes, rules, and preferences is one way of establishing who they are *not*. Most important, they are not like you, parents! Don't take this personally by any means, but rather as the ongoing work of a personality under construction. The peer group becomes supremely important at this age. Again, this focus on peer relationships is normal at this stage of development and should not be misinterpreted as a rejection of the parents or family. Older adolescents in particular need to develop their own style of how they look and behave. This is not an "in your face" message of rejection to the parents, but a decision made to define "who I am."

Teaching Responsibility

We all want our children to be responsible. Responsibility is a quality associated with almost every positive and desirable trait or outcome one can think of: being successful, trustworthy, dependable, predictable, likable, all require a degree of being responsible. The person who is "irresponsible" will likely not achieve a high level of success, nor earn the acceptance and goodwill of others. Responsibility is not something we are born with however. The familiar parental lament that "my kid is just not responsible" is very true. Children by nature are spontaneous, selfish, and interested in immediate gratification rather than working for long-term goals. By definition that makes them "irresponsible," but also normal for a young child.

In his book *Between Parent and Child,* Dr. Haim Ginott makes the sensible observation that responsibility evolves over time, as the child matures: "Responsibility, like piano playing, is attained slowly and over many long years. It requires a daily practice in exercising judgment and in making choices about matters appropriate to one's age and comprehension." Developing responsibility requires complex learned attitudes and behaviors. These involve acquiring a set of beliefs, expectations, and attitudes about ourselves and the way we want to behave. Next comes learning behaviors that make us act in a productive, consistent, "responsible" manner, and repeating those behaviors over time until they become ingrained in our habits and routines. Clearly this does not come from giving the child a lecture, but from teaching the child how to behave when faced with life's many challenges. This takes patience and repeated lessons.

There Are Two Major Ways to Teach Children Responsibility First, we need to allow them choices that are appropriate for them to make so that they learn what helps them and what doesn't, what produces results and what doesn't, what they like and what they don't. The second major method for teaching responsibility is to model it in our own behavior. When a child is faced with making a choice in behavior, the question that will likely come up is not "what did mom or dad say about this?" but rather "how did mom or dad act in this situation?" The question does not require verbalization— the child will model or imitate the behavior she or he observed the parent doing earlier. The modeling effect is so powerful that children will imitate a parents' behavior, or that of another role model, months or even many years after observing the behavior. Is it any coincidence that parents who tend to act responsibly have children who also tend to act responsibly? The reverse is also likely to apply.

Bedtimes, Curfews, Pets, Allowances, Cars

Bedtimes These should be set for kids of all ages, and enforced consistently. Older children will often request, and get, a little later bedtime. Younger siblings may complain, but they understand the fairness of this, and will look forward to "graduating" to a later bedtime as they get older.

Curfews These are set by the legal requirements cities impose, and also by the limits parents impose. The legal curfew does not have to be the standard for the family, or even for the individual teenager or child. Some are more responsible than others, and can handle more freedom. For a high school student, a week-day curfew of 11:00 P.M. would be considered reasonable in the summer, but not during the school year. A midnight curfew on Friday and Saturday nights is pretty standard for responsible adolescents. If curfew is violated, that freedom gets restricted for a while. Dr. Thomas Phelan, author of the very practical book *Surviving Your Adolescents,* recommends a fifteen-minute grace period. After fifteen minutes, the teen should "pay back" the time by coming in earlier the next time she or he goes out. After forty-five minutes, the adolescent pays back double the time. If three hours late or longer, he or she is grounded for a week, or given a consequence of similar severity. These are realistic standards for parents to follow.

Children Love Pets   Be it a gerbil, goldfish, snake, or puppy dog, pets are interesting, fun, cute, and they "belong" to the child. The problem is that most children, particularly young children before the middle teens, are just not capable of taking care of a pet on their own on a consistent basis. The result is that usually the parent ends up taking responsibility for keeping the pet alive. As long as this is understood, then allowing the child to have a pet is just fine.

Allowances   Getting a small allowance allows the child to have some spending money, and also provides the opportunity to learn how to manage money. By providing freedom and choices in this area, the child learns how to handle money responsibly or else learns "how quickly money goes." It should be understood that an allowance is not a reward for doing chores, or for good behavior. It is given because the child is part of the family. Threats of "you will lose your allowance" for misbehaving defeats its purpose entirely. Other consequences should be used to deal with bad behavior, such as restricting freedoms or privileges.

Car Privileges   Few things have the potential to cause as much strife between parents and older teens as driving and having access to a car. The rules and expectations around car privileges need to be made clear, then followed. When can the adolescent use the car, and for what purposes? What are the teen's responsibilities in paying for gas? How about car insurance? Many adolescents share expenses for gas, and pay for half or all of their car insurance, particularly when the parents have limited finances. Some of the more mature, resourceful teens manage to earn and save enough money to buy their own car. Who sets the rules then? The parents do, as long as the child is a minor and living in the house. The teenager responsible enough to accomplish that feat may also be quite responsible about using the car as well.

Kids Never Had It So Good—Or Do They?

Lets face it, parents are busy these days. Our jobs are demanding, traffic is a killer, we have to get our taxes done by the fifteenth, and the roof is leaking again. When life gets too hectic and you've missed another of your daughter's basketball games, it's easy to fall prey to guilt feelings. You know that she wants the new Princess Betsy Dream Boat Vacation Cruise package, the one with the two-foot-long plastic boat. She's only been talking about if for the past three weeks, right? The next thing you know, you are pulling the car into the toy store parking lot.

Parental Guilt? Perhaps, but also the influence of a materialistic culture where, we are convinced, it takes the new hot product on the market to make us happy. We want our children to be happy, and they are only too eager to let us know what they want. Have kids ever gotten as many material possessions as they do these days? One gets the impression that no child is complete without the video game console, portable CD player, stereo in the bedroom (and increasingly, a computer), roller-blades, and bike in the garage.

There seems little doubt that children get more these days than kids have ever gotten before. This is not the children's fault of course—kids will be kids, and will want what they want because a friend has it, they saw it on TV, or they saw it advertised in a magazine. It is the parents' job to set limits, not to expect the kids to set those limits. What many parents are asking themselves is, are we giving too much? When does it become *too much,* and what are the effects of all this generosity?

The discomforting feeling for many parents is that of raising a generation of children who are becoming bored and jaded with everything that is given to them. Human nature being what it is, when things come too easily, without any need to earn them or work for them, they lose value in our eyes. When indulgent parents give their children so much in material goods and privileges, sometimes before the kids even ask for or want them, what does that do to a person's work ethic? If what I want is given to me, where is the value of working to achieve my goals?

Overdone Generosity   This can set up expectations of entitlement. A sense of entitlement in turn kills any incentives to work for the things we want. Children, as well as adults, can become jaded and bored when there are no challenges to conquer, no goals to shoot for. After the computer at twelve and the sports car at sixteen, what is next? Where is the next thrill going to come from? Many anxious parents don't even want to think about those answers. For many of the more affluent kids living in suburbia and the wealthier areas in large cities, the kick may come from designer drugs, drinking, and sex. These are larger issues, and important ones indeed, for parents to consider as they make decisions about freedoms and responsibilities and communicate with their children about these questions. There are no set, cookie-cutter answers.

Chapter **24**

Deal with the Tough Issues: Drinking, Drugs, Sex, AIDS

B eing only human (like their parents), children and adolescents get into trouble at times. They make poor decisions, act impulsively, and generally get themselves into situations they later wish could have been avoided. Some problems are fairly minor, such as getting a detention for talking back to a teacher, or lying about having done a chore, and these can be dealt with without long-lasting damage. Other mistakes can cause serious and lasting legal, educational, financial, or health problems.

DON'T AVOID THE TOUGH ISSUES OR THEY COULD TURN INTO BIG PROBLEMS

Every parent has worries about their child being involved with alcohol and other drug abuse, unsafe use of the car, sexually transmitted diseases including AIDS, or unwanted pregnancy. Serious problems, ones that can do real damage to the child and the family, often revolve around substance abuse and irresponsible sexual behavior. Dealing with these problems requires discussion, honest communication, planning and problem solving, and sometimes professional intervention. Ignoring these problems can lead to disaster.

Alcohol and Other Drugs

There are many reasons why adolescents or even preadolescents turn to drug abuse. Alcohol and other drugs are freely available, and teens will find them at parties, friends' houses, and even at school. Some teens are simply bored and turn to drug use for recreational reasons; they want to "see how it feels" and have fun with their peers. Some face emotional problems or fears of failure, and turn to illicit substances to "self-medicate" and anesthetize themselves emotionally. They may experience a good deal of social pressure to conform and be "cool" like everyone else—it is anathema to most adolescents to be "different" from their peers. They fit in by smoking cigarettes, drinking alcohol, or using other types of drugs. For some kids, using alcohol or other drugs gives them a sense of maturity and independence.

Alcohol is the legal and most widely used mood-altering drug of course, but other chemicals are commonly used and cause problems as well. Often these are used in addition to drinking alcohol. As many as 90 percent of high school students use alcohol by the time they graduate (Wilmes, 1988). As many as half of all high school seniors have tried marijuana. Twenty percent may abuse amphetamines, diet pills, caffeine pills, and illegally produced street "speed" such as crystal methedrine. Fifteen percent may try cocaine. Upward of 15 percent may abuse inhalants, such as glue, paint thinner, lighter fluid, or aerosols. Ten percent may use hallucinogens such as LSD or mescaline. Ten percent may abuse minor tranquilizers such as Valium, Xanax, or Ativan. Nine percent may use narcotics such as codeine, Percodan, heroin, and morphine.

Whom Will They Learn From?

Parents need to educate themselves about the risks of substance abuse, and to educate their children about those dangers as well. We live in a culture where children in the fourth grade—yes indeed, fourth graders—are reporting peer pressure to drink alcohol. Education about substance abuse can hardly start too early. It is important for parents to discuss drinking and drug use with their children, beginning in grade school. This should never be treated as a taboo topic, or avoided due to the parents' discomfort with the issue.

Learning About Substance Abuse   If your children don't learn bout substance abuse from you the parent, they will learn about it from someone else. If they don't receive rules, values, and expectations about their own use of alcohol and other drugs from parents and family, they will develop values and expectations from other sources. They will be exposed to drugs, and will be prepared to deal with those situations from a position of knowledge and healthy expectations, or from a position of naïveté and uncertainty. What do you want your children to know about drugs, and how do you want them to behave? Teach them those things. Even the parents who take the stance that "kids will be kids" still need to educate their children about the dangers of drinking and drug use. Don't assume your children are splashing around in the mud puddle when they may be hip deep in the quicksand pit.

Substance abuse not only imperils a person's health, but his life as well. Rules about drinking need to be made very clear, limits established and enforced, and problems dealt with quickly if they come up. Most parents will simply not tolerate any use of alcohol or other drugs before the age of sixteen. Many teens will experiment with alcohol during the high school years, perhaps having the occasional beer or drink at a party with their peers. Some parents consider it all right to allow their teen a beer or glass of wine at home, as long as the teen does not drive afterward. Every parent must determine their own tolerance and comfort level for such social drinking, and set the rules accordingly with their own children.

If the substance abuse becomes a problem, then it's time to work with a substance abuse counselor or other mental health professional. Sometimes outpatient substance abuse counseling and support groups are all that's needed, and sometimes inpatient treatment in a hospital or residential treatment center is required. The child or teen does not have to agree to such treatment, if he is in danger. With sufficient cause, which a physician or other health professional can help determine, parents have the right to hospitalize their child before the age of eighteen.

Dangerous Situations   It is a dangerous situation   for parents to deny a substance abuse problem when it exists. This is not a time to shy away from conflicts, worry about "what will the relatives think," blame oneself for the child's problems, or attempt to "rescue" the child by saving them from the consequences of their behavior. Parents who try to protect their children from the problems associated with their substance abuse become enablers, and unwittingly contribute to the problem and help to perpetuate it. Making excuses for the child, lying to others, doing the child's work for them, and keeping the substance abuse problem a secret from family members or health care professionals are all examples of enabling behaviors that end up making the problem worse. In the story which follows, Jason's well-meaning and too forgiving parents show the roles that denial and enabling can play in the life of a teen with a drinking problem.

Jason's Story

When I met Jason he was eighteen and had recently smashed up his second sports car. He was halfway through his senior year of high school, a star on the football team, friendly and personable, liked by everyone. Jason was an average student in high school, although he had achieved higher grades up until eighth grade. At the age of fifteen he was caught smoking marijuana in his parents' basement along with some friends. This led to a long discussion and being grounded for a week. They saw a family therapist for two sessions, then the parents considered the matter resolved. Jason's parents were wealthy and generous to him. He was a young man who pretty much got whatever he wanted, and he used his charm to persuade his parents and others.

For his sixteenth birthday Jason's parents gave him a new red sports car that he'd talked about for the previous year. He became even more popular among his peers and enjoyed his status immensely. He went to all the parties, he was a sports star, and he was drinking more along with a core group of friends. Ten months after getting the car he drove home late from a party, hit a patch of ice, went into a very bad skid, and overturned the car into a ditch. He had been smart enough to wear his seat belt, which undoubtedly saved his life. His parents found out details about the party and Jason's drinking, and were understandably upset. They knew he had been drinking and admonished him for it, but ultimately had accepted it as something that teenage boys did.

The parents next took Jason to see a substance abuse counselor who recommended counseling and a support group. Jason went for several sessions, but found that he didn't like the counselor, and then he started missing sessions. His parents were busy with work, and they could not attend regular sessions either. After awhile the sessions stopped, as did involvement in the support group. Jason's parents did not see any signs of continued drinking or other drug use. His grades improved a little as well. They surprised Jason by buying him another new car for his seventeenth birthday. He reassured them that he was being responsible and staying sober.

The reality was that Jason had gotten very good at hiding his drinking and marijuana use from his parents. He was getting high mostly at parties, sometimes three or four times per week. His grades were dropping again, but he rationalized that it didn't matter. He knew he was not going to get into one of the top colleges, and he could always get into a less prestigious one. He was not concerned about the future, but rather about enjoying himself in the present. His parents took pride in his athletic accomplishments and his social popularity.

The second car accident happened on the way to school. Jason sped up to make it through a yellow light and just caught it when it turned red. Another car was hurrying to make a left-hand turn and turned right into Jason's path. Fortunately neither driver was seriously injured, but both cars were wrecked. Jason came to his first appointment wearing a neck brace. Despite that, he was in a good mood, and able to laugh at himself and his bad luck. His parents were more somber. He had been late for school too often, the mother explained, and was rushing to make it to his first class on time. They were concerned about Jason's poor driving and the obvious dangers that posed to his safety. They were also concerned about his erratic academic performance.

The reason Jason was running late that morning was because he had been out well after midnight the night before. He had gone to a friend's house to watch a movie and had "a couple of beers." As Jason's history and recent behavior became more clear after a few sessions, it became obvious that both he and his parents were in denial about the extent and severity of his substance abuse problem. This was a young person who had been a good student prior to age fourteen. The substance abuse began then and had gotten progressively worse. In recent months he was smoking marijuana and drinking alcohol three or four days per week. He needed more intensive intervention to treat the substance abuse than he'd had previously. An inpatient substance abuse program at a hospital with a good reputation was recommended, to be followed up by intensive outpatient treatment and support groups.

Jason flatly refused to consider this option and considered it totally unnecessary. His accidents were not caused by substance abuse, but rather an icy road and a bad decision while rushing to get to school. His parents seemed torn between giving him the treatment he needed but also not compounding the problem, as they saw it. They acknowledged his problem with alcohol but did not consider him an "alcoholic." A history of inpatient substance abuse treatment would reflect badly on him, hurt his reputation in the community (and that of the parents as well), and damage his opportunities for college. Wouldn't more frequent outpatient sessions be enough? The realistic answer was: no.

Jason's parents decided to work with another therapist whom they considered more flexible. That treatment lasted for several weeks, then became sporadic and ended when Jason went away to college. This author met the father at a social occasion after Jason's first semester in college. Jason had been drinking heavily since school began, stopped going to classes, and dropped out when the semester ended. He moved back home with his parents and was working for his father. He was also working with a substance abuse counselor and attending Alcoholics Anonymous groups. He was on his third sports car, because he needed transportation for work.

Would the inpatient program have made a difference for Jason, the father asked? There was no way to know for certain, of course. What we know about substance abuse problems, however, is that without aggressive and effective treatment they get progressively worse. Staying in denial about the problem almost always makes it worse.

Reducing the Risk The good news about substance abuse is that parents can make a difference in reducing the "risk factors" that make children more likely to escalate drinking or other drug use to the point that it becomes a real problem. Psychological research has shown that teens who use substances frequently tend to have higher levels of stress, cannot cope as well with their problems, have academic difficulties as early as junior high school, and have lower levels of parental support. Parents can help reduce these risk factors by listening and trying to understand their child, being supportive, and providing help for academic or learning problems. Children can be taught how to consider options, think about long-term consequences of behavior, and make responsible decisions. They can also be taught to resist offers from peers, and to put advertising and media images about drinking, smoking, and drug use into perspective.

If substance abuse itself is the problem, then of course substance abuse treatment needs to become part of the solution. It is important to find a counselor or therapist with training and experience in the field of chemical dependence. No parent should ever give up hope or throw up their hands in frustration in the face of alcohol or other drug problems. Such problems are treatable, and usually the sooner the better. Finally, it is imperative that the parents seek help for themselves if they have a problem with substance abuse. Lectures, threats, and rules about substance abuse will fall on deaf teenage ears if the parent is hypocritical about her own behavior.

Sex, AIDS, and Pregnancy

The age-old advice on sexuality from parents to teens and young adults used to be "don't have sex until you get married." That changed over the past twenty or thirty years to "don't have sex, but if you do don't get pregnant." Now the message is more like "don't have sex, but if you do don't get AIDS and don't get pregnant." If this seems confusing for parents, imagine what it must sound like to teens and young adults. They hear messages about morality and abstinence from some sources, which translates into "no sex." Other messages are about avoiding dangers, which translates into having "safe sex." At the same time, they are constantly exposed to sexual messages and images in the popular culture and the media, which implicitly says "yes" to sex. Add to that the normal adolescent hormonal drives, along with peer pressure, and you have a confusing jumble of conflicting messages and influences.

Most children become sexually aware, and more curious, during the middle school years. This is a good time for discussions about the facts and issues surrounding sexuality, although some parents prefer to hold conversations about sexuality when the children are even younger. Adolescents reaching puberty are not only very curious about their sexual development, but often quite anxious about it as well. They wonder if they are developing "normally," or (horrors!) "too slow." They need to understand that changes in puberty vary among individuals, and that each person develops at his or her own pace. Physical changes that occur with the onset of puberty need to be accepted as natural, biological processes, and not teased about or belittled. Girls in particular need understanding and reassurance when they begin menstruating. Most girls experience menstrual pain and cramping when they begin to have their cycles, and need to be supported by parents and teachers alike during periods of physical discomfort. Just as important, they need to be aware of the changes their bodies are going through and not fear these changes.

Value Issues and the Family

Teens need to have information and basic knowledge about pregnancy, childbirth, contraception, and sexually transmitted diseases. Teachers and parents can both deal with these straightforward, fact-based issues. Adolescence is also a crucial time to discuss the values, morality, and expectations about sexual behavior. The value issues are best communicated between parents and children, and not necessarily in a sex education class at school.

Those parents who worry that knowledge about contraceptives might give the child a message that "it's okay to have sex," and thus encourage the child to become sexually active, need to know that those fears are unfounded. Those parents should consider, in addition, that the price children pay for their ignorance about contraceptives might be their lives if they contract AIDS. How many parents are truly willing to take that risk? How many adolescents *should* be willing to take such a risk? The reasonable answer, in the age of AIDS, is "none." Teaching sexual abstinence in adolescence has many things to recommend it, however there are no guarantees that the teens will be responsible enough and strong enough to practice it. Even if abstinence until marriage (or at least until adulthood) is taught as a value, knowledge about contraceptives and discussions about responsible behavior always need to be part of the equation.

Teen Sex and Pregnancy The effects of peer pressure and media images on sexual behavior, and the consequences of teenage pregnancy, all need to be discussed openly and realistically. A dialogue which flows in both directions is infinitely more effective than a lecture from an adult to a teen. Beyond communication and information, teens need acceptance and support from family and other adults in their lives. Teens who feel insecure and unloved are more likely to give in to peer pressure and become sexually active. This is where the family again plays such a crucial role in providing acceptance and love, and in shaping expectations, values, and behavior.

Few things can so profoundly affect the course of a life, or two people's lives (or three), as a teen pregnancy. Typically, the pregnancies are unintentional, but sometimes they are planned. As difficult as it might be for adults to understand, some girls decide to get pregnant and have a child because they feel lonely and want the child for companionship. Having a baby is not, of course, a *solution* for feeling lonely or unloved. Developing caring relationships with peers and adults would be a much more practical, responsible, and healthy solution. Children should not be having children, for emotional reasons as well as for the obvious financial reasons and the practical and physical responsibilities involved in raising a child. Teen pregnancy causes problems for teens and babies. For that reason, many teens choose to give up the baby for adoption, or to have an abortion.

What are reasonable expectations for adolescents around the issues of dating, relationships with the opposite sex, and sexuality? Most teens before the age of sixteen prefer going out with a group of friends as opposed to going out on a date as a couple. Most parents feel safer with this type of arrangement as well. Many parents would set limits on having a girl under the age of sixteen going in a car by herself with a boy old enough to drive. Expectations need to be discussed related to celibacy and sexual behavior, for both males and females. This is not a time to further sexual stereotypes, where boys are expected to be sexually active while girls are expected to protect their virtue. Responsible, healthy behaviors seldom go along with gender stereotypes.

Chapter **25**

Parents and Grown Children: Caring Without Meddling

A s soon as a child is born, being a parent becomes a lifetime role. A parent-child relationship evolves over time, as the needs of the child and the responsibilities of the parent both change over the years. Under the right circumstances, the relationship remains among the most important emotional and intimate relationship for both. Under the "wrong" circumstances, the relationship becomes strained and difficult. For some people, tragically, the relationship becomes severed. How many parents grow old feeling unappreciated and neglected by the adult children they worked so hard to raise? How many adult children keep a distance, nursing old wounds and striving to maintain a sense of independence and freedom? The answer to both questions is, too many.

DON'T NEGLECT OR TRY TO CONTROL YOUR GROWN CHILD

This chapter is addressed to parents with grown children, and also to the adult children who may themselves be parents. We have reached a point in the book, as people reach a point in their lives, where parents and children truly become equals in terms of responsibility and influence on each other. This chapter is not so much about teaching, guiding, and helping, but rather about mutual acceptance and support. Even those areas can become problematic, however. When teaching, helping, or even support become unwelcome and intrusive, they turn into the dreaded "meddling." Now there is a word guaranteed to raise the blood pressure on both sides!

The challenges for an elderly parent with grown children are many in maintaining and nurturing a relationship with an adult child. Where is the fine line between doing too little or too much? Where does caring end and meddling begin? At the same time, the resources for parents with adult children are few. How many books and articles have been written on the topic of parenting young children? Bookstores and library shelves are filled with them. The motivated and resourceful parent can learn all about the developmental stages of childhood, the problems to expect and how to deal with them, and 1,001 tips on how to improve their parenting skills. One book alone offers *Good Behavior: Over 1,200 Sensible Solutions To Your Child's Problems From Birth To Age Twelve* (Garber et al., 1987). Twelve hundred sensible solutions for dealing with young children? How about twelve sensible solutions, some parents may wonder, for dealing with a grown child? Keep on reading—this chapter will provide exactly that.

Out of Sight, but Close to the Heart

One of the joys of parenting is playing a part in the everyday lives of children. We watch them grow and mature, change diapers, wipe runny noses, share in their excitement of learning and discovery, anguish over problems and pain, and celebrate successes. We are there with them, continuously involved in what is happening in their lives. All of that changes profoundly when the grown child moves out and makes a home, family, and life of their own. The "apron strings" hopefully have been cut in terms of the child assuming responsibility, and the parent feeling less of a need to guide or influence their children's lives further.

Sometimes the apron strings are *not* cut, which no doubt will continue to cause untold problems for both parent and child. These are the situations where "meddling" truly applies, with all its noxious ramifications. Some parents wish to maintain influence in their children's lives because they are overly controlling, or cannot bear the separation from the child which independence implies. Some children, on the other hand, may not want the apron strings cut either because they are overly dependent on the parent and insecure about their own ability to live independent lives. Neither situation is a healthy one, and countless therapy sessions have been spent discussing them.

The more common occurrence, however, is for a parent, caring and well-meaning in every sense, to struggle to be helpful and supportive while having limited knowledge about what goes on in the adult child's life and the things they may need help with. Sometimes the needs are obvious and easily communicated from child to parent, such as advice on buying a house or a loan to furnish a new apartment after college graduation. Sometimes the problems are very personal and covered with shame and guilt, such as the child who develops a substance abuse problem, or has job and marital problems. The parent may easily sense that a problem exists, and have limited knowledge about the situation. What to do then? How to help, or try to help, and not meddle? As Betty Frain and Eileen Clegg write so succinctly in their book *Becoming A Wise Parent For Your Grown Child*, "it takes creativity, self-awareness, and often a saintlike tolerance for ambiguity if parents are to maintain healthy relationships with their grown kids." And you thought the hard work was done after they passed the teenage years?

The Myth of the Controlling Parent, Mean Mother-In-Law, and Generation Gap

We have all heard the mother-in-law jokes and stories. You know, that nosy, meddling, critical, controlling woman who raised your spouse and now can't stand you? How terrible and unfair those jokes are. "Take my mother-in-law—please!" I have a mother-in-law named Jacqueline, and she is one of the kindest, gentlest people on the face of the earth. I will take her any day of the week as a relative, a pleasant person to be around, a great cook, a delight to her grandchildren, and a wise confidante to many people in her large extended family. She has done a wonderful job raising her children, who would be foolish indeed to distance themselves in the name of being independent. Most parents are much like Jacqueline, not intrusive or controlling ogres but caring and well-meaning people. My parents, Matei and Anuica, are the same, as is my father-in-law Dominick. Where then do the stereotypes come from, that mother-in-laws are pests, and that parents can't wait to meddle and control their children's lives? There is a cultural expectation that parents and grown children are somehow caught up in a generation gap and cannot communicate or get along with each other. This is nonsense, and even worse, it's harmful nonsense. It creates expectations for conflict, resentment, and hostility.

The larger truth is that most parents continue to care and be concerned about their children no matter what their age, or their status as independent adults. Care and concern do not translate into being controlling or meddling, of course. The sad thing is that many parents are simply afraid to show their concern, or ask normal questions about their children and their families, without being perceived as intruding. Parents become reticent about asking questions, and children become defensive when asked. Under a policy of "don't meddle," many parents decide to ignore even serious problems they see going on with their children or grandchildren. Is this any way for mature, loving adults to behave? Popular self-help books discuss the dangers of "toxic parents" and "toxic families." If you listen to the TV talk shows, every person in this country grew up in a "dysfunctional family" it seems, with the exception perhaps of some guy who was raised by wolves in northern Minnesota. The cultural stereotypes become self-fulfilling prophesies, to everyone's loss. We lose the wisdom of our elderly parents, who too often drift away into isolation themselves. This is a tragedy, and a foolish and needless one at that.

The most "toxic" or "dysfunctional" thing going on may be the stereotypes themselves, and the way they are repeated and hyped in the popular media. Turn off the TV talk show, close your self-help book, and take a look at your parents. These are the people who loved and raised you since you were born, most certainly meaning well and doing the best they could. How "toxic" are they? Lifetime relationships don't happen without conflicts and hurts, but that is no reason to withdraw from family or relegate parents to the roles of potential meddlers and troublemakers.

Twelve Sensible Rules for Parents of Adult Children

There are certain basic principles and rules that apply to making any adult relationship work. Mutual respect is essential, along with consideration and sensitivity to others. Honesty and trust build a base for cooperation and intimacy. A caring, helpful attitude can be very comforting, particularly during times of trouble. A parent-child relationship is like no other, even in adulthood, in terms of the richness of its history and the depth of feelings. Following is a list of a dozen rules and principles for parents with grown children. These define some, but by no means all, of the important characteristics of a close parent-child relationship in adulthood. These simply serve as a good foundation.

1. *Acknowledge and appreciate the individual.* Can you truly appreciate the person that your child has become? If so, express that, directly and with genuine appreciation and affection. Most of us walk around with some apprehension about being disappointed by the people who mean the most to us. Don't let your children think that about you. Parents, too, need to hear words of acknowledgment, appreciation, and thanks as well.

2. *Your caring never ends, but your responsibility does.* Most parents consider their responsibility for their children to end around the time the child finishes college. At that point, the apron strings must indeed be cut, not by cutting off the person but by allowing the person to make their own important decisions in life. These include where to live, what job to take, whom to marry, and so on. The child will never become a fully mature, responsible adult until he assumes responsibility for his behavior and the major decisions in his life. The parent who tries to intrude or interfere with these major decisions, without being asked for her opinion and having her opinion welcomed, is guilty of the dreaded "meddling."

3. *Don't take on guilt for your children's mistakes or failures.* You can influence but cannot control what your children do, not in childhood and certainly not in adulthood. The child you raised is a thinking, feeling, acting human being who will make his own decisions in adult life. When the person makes bad decisions and ends up in trouble, the fault is not yours. You did not "fail" the child, and no guilt is deserved on the part of the parent.

4. *Be a sounding board, not a megaphone.* Parents make wonderful sounding boards and sources of feedback, when their children ask for their opinion and are open to them. They make terrible megaphones, which is what happens when they lecture or try to force their views and ideas on the children. Lecturing didn't work or help when the children were young. What makes you think they will work now? Help them find answers by listening attentively, brainstorm for ideas if necessary, but don't lecture or preach.

5. *Give of yourself most of all.* Share what you know and what you experienced. One of the best ways to teach a lesson is to talk about how a lesson affected us, because that helps to make it personal and more real for the listener. Did you also have trouble with a difficult boss? Flunked a course in college? Share those experiences with your child who may be going through a

similar situation. The child is now an adult and can see you in a very different light, as a real person, warts and all. Be honest, because honesty begets trust which begets further honesty. One of the benefits of age is wisdom, and one benefit of wisdom is a profound appreciation for the truth. Teach this principle by living it out in your own life, and expressing it in your communications with your grown children. Role modeling doesn't stop when they go away to college.

6. *Accept and appreciate differences.* Your children have your genes and the benefits of your teaching, but they are not you. They will develop their own tastes, styles, and beliefs. Their values and goals may not be even similar to the values you taught them and the goals you hoped they would pursue. How strong then is your ability to accept their differences? Families have been torn apart over their stand on abortion issues, civil rights, women's rights, or something as ridiculous as how a person voted in a presidential election. What if your child is gay? The choices parents face are to accept the person for who they are, or to practice intolerance and rejection. Having different beliefs, values, or orientations than you is not a matter of disloyalty or disrespect. Grown children owe their parents respect, certainly. Affection is earned rather than owed, but even in difficult relationships this is usually not a problem after a lifetime of caretaking and nurturing. What your children don't owe you, nor anyone else, are their values and beliefs. That's what being an independent adult living in a free society implies, the freedom to think and choose for oneself. The parent who cannot accept that, and thus cannot accept their child's differences, is the one who is choosing to reject and distance.

7. *Don't rehash old hurts and grievances.* People who live in the past typically look back on problems, failures, and disappointments, not on positive memories or feelings. This is a recipe for anger, resentment, and often, depression. Children who blame their parents for some past hurt, an unhappy childhood, or a failure

in their lives, are the ones most likely to distance themselves in anger or even break off the relationship with the parent. It is healthier to forgive one another, and forget. If the child is the one who is not forgiving, let him know that you're ready to have a relationship again. It may not happen right away, but at some point down the road reconciliation is probably possible.

8. *Don't let the children meddle in your life.* Although parents have the stereotyped reputation for being the meddlers, the other side of the coin is the child who intrudes into the parent's life. This is even more likely to happen if one of the parents becomes widowed or divorced, or if the child has difficulty breaking away from the parents. Assert your rights to live your life the way you want, spend your money the way you want, and be involved with people you want to be involved with. What's fair is fair, in both directions.

9. *Keep your financial involvement minimal.* Shakespeare's advice to "neither a borrower nor a lender be" is difficult to live by these days in our easy credit society. The principle is important when it comes to parents and grown children however. Even the adult child still living at home should be expected to be an adult, and thus responsible for her financial needs. Financial assistance to get a young adult situated in a job or new home is one thing, but not continued financial support from the parents. The most common type of dependency is financial, and characteristic of the child who wants to cling to a needy child role. Establishing an income is important, as well as a credit rating, and the ability to secure a loan from a bank when necessary. If the adult child needs to borrow money from you to buy a boat, it probably means that he can't afford the boat.

10. *Intervene in life-threatening situations.* There are times when a parent, or any responsible family member for that matter, must take quick action to deal with a dangerous situation where the life or safety of a child or grandchild is at stake. These include

situations where the parents discover or strongly suspect that child abuse is going on, or domestic violence, the threat of suicide or homicide, severe depression or other mental illness, and substance abuse when the abuse is threatening the safety of the adult or children being cared for by the adult. The issue of being intrusive or meddling becomes a moot point in those situations. Abuse and violence cannot be tolerated. A person having suicidal or homicidal thoughts or impulses is a clear danger, and needs immediate psychiatric care. A parent who is using dangerous drugs is a danger to himself, and also a danger to children if the parent drives them around while intoxicated. If the adult child will not take meaningful, responsible action right away to help herself, the parents can turn to their doctor for advice, call a crisis hotline, or call the local police department and seek immediate assistance.

11. *Respect your children's parental authority.* Parents set the rules and expectations for their children, not the grandparents. That applies even when the grandchildren are visiting your house. There is no more certain way to step on toes and make your adult children feel defensive than to criticize their childrearing methods. Entering a dispute between a parent and child on the side of the child is asking for trouble, and certainly an inappropriate challenge to the parents' authority. Spoiling the grandkids a little is usually harmless and can be lots of fun, but be sensitive to any complaints the parents might have that you could be spoiling them too much. If that's the case, respect their wishes.

12. *Share responsibility for the quality of your relationship.* Equal rights, status, and freedom in an adult relationship also imply equal responsibility. The relationship between a parent and young child must often be shaped by the parent, for obvious reasons. The relationship with a grown child must be shared, with each giving support, communicating what they need, and making decisions on a shared basis. Expect that they will be as honest and open with you as you are with them, and will make

efforts to keep the family ties strong. Share responsibility for the well-being of relationships with them, your own and those within the larger family as well, and your children truly become your equals.

INTO THE FUTURE

1. Acknowledge and appreciate the individual.
2. Your caring never ends, but your responsibility does.
3. Don't take on guilt for your children's mistakes or failures.
4. Be a sounding board, not a megaphone.
5. Give of yourself most of all.
6. Accept and appreciate differences.
7. Don't rehash old hurts and grievances.
8. Don't let the children meddle in your life.
9. Keep your financial involvement minimal.
10. Intervene in life-threatening situations.
11. Respect your children's parental authority.
12. Share responsibility for the quality of your relationship.

Appendix

Resources and Organizations for Parents and Families

Attention Deficit Disorder

C.H.A.D.D.
8181 Professional Place, Suite 201
Landover, MD 20785
www.chadd.org

National Attention Deficit Disorder Association
P.O. Box 1303
Northbrook, IL 60015-1303
www.add.org

Child Abuse

Child-Help U.S.A. Child Abuse
P.O. Box 630
Los Angeles, CA 90028
Hotline: 1-800-422-4453

Depression

National Alliance For The Mentally Ill
200 North Glebe Road, Suite 1015
Arlington, VA 22203-3754
(703) 524-7600

Divorce

American Arbitration Association
140 West 51st Street
New York, NY 10020-1203

Domestic Violence

National Coalition Against Domestic Violence
Hotline: 1-800-799-7233

Drug and Alcohol Abuse

Alcoholics Anonymous
P.O. Box 459
Grand Central Station
New York, NY 10163

American Council For Drug Education
164 West 74th Street
New York, NY 10023
1-800-488-DRUG

Eating Disorders

American Anorexia/Bulimia Association
133 Cedar Lane
Teaneck, NJ 07666

Gay and Lesbian

Federation of Parents and Friends of Lesbians and Gays
1101 14th Street NW, Suite 1030
Washington, DC 20005
(202) 638-4200

Grandparents

American Association For Retired People
Grandparent Information Center
601 E. Street NW
Washington, DC 20049
(202) 434-2277

Legal Information

American Bar Association
750 Lake Shore Drive
Chicago, IL 60611
(312) 988-5000

Mental Health

National Mental Health Association
1-800-336-1114

Single Parents

Parents Without Partners
7910 Woodmont Avenue
Bethesda, MD 20814

Stepparents

Step Parent Association of America
28 Allegheny Avenue, Suite 1307
Baltimore, MD 21204

References

Bettelheim, B. *A Good Enough Parent.* New York: Alfred A. Knopf, 1988.

Caissy, G. *Early Adolescence: Understanding the 10- to 15-Year-Old.* New York: Plenum Press, 1994.

Coles, R. *The Spiritual Life of Children.* Boston: Houghton Mifflin, 1990.

Curran, D. *Traits of a Healthy Family.* New York: Ballantine Books, 1983.

Dinkmeyer, D. and McKay, G. *Raising a Responsible Child.* New York: Fireside Books, 1996.

Dodson, F. *How to Single Parent.* New York: Harper & Row, 1987.

Einstein, E. and Albert, L. *Strengthening Your Stepfamily.* Circle Pines, Minn.: American Guidance Services, 1986.

Elkind, D. *The Hurried Child: Growing Up Too Fast Too Soon.* New York: Addison Wesley Longman, Inc., 1989.

Faber, A. and Mazlish, E. *How to Talk So Kids Will Listen & Listen So Kids Will Talk.* New York: Avon Books, 1982.

————. E. *Siblings Without Rivalry.* New York: Avon Books, 1987.

Felner, R.D., et al. "A Life Transition Framework for Understanding Marital Dissolution and Family Reorganization." In A. Wolchik and P. Karoly (eds.), *Children of Divorce: Empirical Perspective on Adjustment.* New York: 1988.

Frain, B. and Clegg, E. *Becoming a Wise Parent for Your Grown Child.* Oakland, Calif.: New Harbinger Publications, 1997.

Garber, S., et al. *Good Behavior: Over 1,200 Sensible Solutions to Your Child's Problems from Birth to Age Twelve.* New York: St. Martin's Paperbacks, 1987.

Gardner, R. *The Boys and Girls Book About Divorce.* New York: Bantam Books, 1988.

Ginott, H. *Between Parent and Child.* New York: Avon Books, 1965.

Hallowell, E. *When You Worry About the Child You Love.* New York: Simon & Schuster, 1996.

Lewis, C. *Listening to Children.* North Vale, NJ: Jason Aronson, 1992.

Lewinsohn, P., et al. Age-cohort: Changes in the Lifetime Occurrence of Depression and Other Mental Disorders. *The Journal of Abnormal Psychology.*

Miller, A. *The Drama of the Gifted Child.* New York: Basic Books, 1981.

Mussen, P., et al. *Child Development and Personality.* New York: Harper & Row, 1984.

Nadeau, K. *Help4ADD@HighSchool.* Bethesda, Md.: Advantage Books, 1998.

Phelan, T. *1-2-3 Magic.* Glen Ellen, Ill.: Child Management Inc., 1990.

———. *Surviving Your Adolescents.* Glen Ellen, Ill.: Child Management Inc., 1991.

Piaget, J. *The Moral Judgment of the Child.* New York: The Free Press, 1965.

Pipher, M. *Reviving Ophelia: Saving the Selves of Adolescent Girls.* New York: Ballantine Books, 1994.

Sandler, I.N., et al. "The Stressors of Children's Postdivorce Environments." In A. Wolchik and P. Karoly (Eds.), *Children of Divorce: Empirical Perspectives on Adjustment.* New York: Gardner Press, 1988.

Seligman, M. *The Optimistic Child.* New York: HarperCollins Publishers, 1996.

Setley, S. *Taming the Dragons: Real Help for Real School Problems.* St. Louis, Mo.: Starfish Publishing, 1995.

Shure, M. and DiGeronimo, F. *Raising a Thinking Child.* New York: Pocket Books, 1994.

Silberman, M. and Wheelan, S. *How to Discipline Without Feeling Guilty.* Champaign, Ill.: Research Press, 1980.

Staudacher, C. *Beyond Grief: A Guide for Recovering from the Death of a Loved One.* Oakland, Calif.: New Harbinger Publications, 1987.

Stern, D. *Diary of a Baby.* New York: Basic Books, 1990.

Twain, H. In *Notes,* reprinted in *601 Quotes About Marriage & Family.* Tyndale House,1998.

Vigna, J. *I Wish Daddy Didn't Drink So Much.* Niles, IL: Albert Whitman & Co., 1988.

Wills, T., et al. "Escalated Substance Use: A Longitudinal Grouping Analysis from Early to Middle Adolescence." *Journal of Abnormal Psychology.*

Wilmes, D. *Parenting for Prevention: How to Raise a Child to Say No to Alcohol/Drugs.* Minneapolis: Johnson Institute Books, 1988.

Wolchick, S. and Karoly, P. *Children of Divorce: Empirical Perspective on Adjustment.* New York: Gardner Press, 1988.

Wyckoff, J. and Unell, B. *Discipline Without Shouting or Spanking.* New York: Meadowbrook Press, 1984.

Zesiewicz, M. *Fast Forwarding Through Childhood.* Santa Monica, Calif.: National Medical Enterprises, 1992.

Index